Change Your Story— Despite the Diagnosis

Living Well with Fibromyalgia and other Mental Health Illness

Brenda Mary Love

BALBOA.
PRESS

A DIVISION OF HAY HOUSE

Balboa Press books may be ordered through booksellers or by contacting:

Balboa Press
A Division of Hay House
1663 Liberty Drive
Bloomington, IN 47403
www.balboapress.com
1 (877) 407-4847

Because of the dynamic nature of the Internet, any web addresses or links contained in this book may have changed since publication and may no longer be valid. The views expressed in this work are solely those of the author and do not necessarily reflect the views of the publisher, and the publisher hereby disclaims any responsibility for them.

The author of this book does not dispense medical advice or prescribe the use of any technique as a form of treatment for physical, emotional, or medical problems without the advice of a physician, either directly or indirectly. The intent of the author is only to offer information of a general nature to help you in your quest for emotional and spiritual well-being. In the event you use any of the information in this book for yourself, which is your constitutional right, the author and the publisher assume no responsibility for your actions.

Any people depicted in stock imagery provided by Getty Images are models, and such images are being used for illustrative purposes only. Certain stock imagery © Getty Images.

Print information available on the last page.

ISBN: 978-1-9822-3318-1 (sc)
ISBN: 978-1-9822-3320-4 (hc)
ISBN: 978-1-9822-3319-8 (e)

Library of Congress Control Number: 2019912531

Balboa Press rev. date: 09/24/2019

CONTENTS

INTRODUCTION

"All dis-case comes from a state of unforgiveness"
so "whenever we are ill, we need to look around
to see who it is that we need to forgive"

A course in miracles.

"Resentment, criticism, guilt and fear come from blaming
others and not taking responsibility for your own experiences."

Louise Hay – Affirmation Cards

This memoir is about living with fibromyalgia and other physical ailments endured on my spiritual journey on earth, for lack of a spiritual path. It is about changing perceptions that are key to the soul's growth and survival. It is about learning to forgive myself and others and appreciating the lessons they've taught me, which have—in most cases—brought blessings with love. It is about my life experiences and attitudes that may have caused and contributed to all the unnecessary pain and depression I've experienced. My realization of my broken self and soul led me to seek spiritual healing, and it has been a journey of finding my true passions and purpose in life, despite the diagnosis of multiple mental illnesses turned physical.

As the saying goes, life experiences have a way of allowing us to become more resilient to survive. Whatever negative experience doesn't kill you will make you stronger. By having faith and knowing of the power of the universe, I've learned to overcome and accept my conditions. I am now living the life of my choosing and have learned the power of gratitude and positive thinking. I choose to be happy because of where I've come from and where I am now, knowing that life is what we make it.

However, as I've always known and recently been reminded, we all create our own reality, and our destiny is in our hands.

As I'm writing this, I am rereading Dr. Wayne Dyer from *Being in Balance: 9 Principles for Creating Habits to Match Your Desires*:

> With everything that has happened to you, you can feel sorry for yourself or treat what has happened as a gift. Everything is either an opportunity to grow or an obstacle to keep you from growing. You get to choose.

Doreen Virtue's audio book *Don't Let Anything Dull Your Sparkle* powerfully reminds me that my exposure to dramas, traumas, and stresses from a very young age and well into my adult life have contributed to my current and past physical, mental, and emotional ailments.

My negative experiences and misfortunes are now considered life lessons learned. I admit that I've lived in the victimhood mentality most of my life and have put up with being mistreated by a few low-vibrational beings, and I forgive them. I now know that they were brought into my life to show me how to become a stronger, more caring and assertive person. I love and admire all my past and current partners, friends, and family and am learning to forgive them for any transgressions and appreciate the love they have shown me.

I am truly thankful for and appreciate those people who have contributed to who I am today. Especially those who have shown me what love and acceptance are. Your thoughtfulness and kindness will always be appreciated by me. I now recognize that love is a choice, and the acts of love are kindness, patience, acceptance, understanding, and—above all—forgiveness.

As I've also come to know from reading Doreen Virtue's book *Assertiveness for Earth Angels* that I was a passive person. She describes passivity as follows:

> Being passive means that you don't acknowledge your feelings to yourself or others. Being passive means that you have numbed your feelings so that you no longer care about yourself, others or the issues of the world. Passive people have run away from responsibility and their emotions by "checking out" through drug use or other addictive behavior, spaciness, depression, isolation, or running from job to job to or relationship to relationship.

After reading this I realized that was me. I didn't acknowledge my feelings and numbed my feelings and just blatantly checked out. But I have become aware of my weaknesses as a spiritual being having a human experience. In our physical existence and am striving to be more assertive in a loving way. This is a famous quote that I've heard repeated by most mystics I've encountered:

We are not physical beings having a spiritual experience, we are spiritual beings having a physical experience.

— Pierre Teilhard de Chardin

We all have choices and can change or begin a new life at any time on our spiritual journey. With love, patience, perseverance, and faith in our spiritual, divine essence, we will continue to strive for a joyous and purposeful life, and I hope to inspire those around me to find the peace and joy that is needed to be healthy and whole again.

With the knowledge and wisdom I've acquired along the way, that began with the medicine wheel, also known as the sacred hoop or sacred circle, and other holistic healing modalities, I am on a road to recovery. By practicing these methods, I've become aware of my own self-healing abilities to help me maintain a balanced, active, fulfilling lifestyle.

As depicted in medicine wheel teachings. Our elders and other spiritual teachers and guides describe that life begins with the four elements, earth, air, water, and fire, and the four parts of our self— mental, emotional, physical, and spiritual—and includes mother earth and father sky. The center of the wheel represents the sacred mystery that, to me, relating it to Feng Shui principals, means health.

The medicine wheel concept from the Native American culture provides a model for who we are as individuals. We have an intellectual (mental) self, a physical self, an emotional self, and a spiritual self. Strength and balance in all quadrants of these can produce a strong, positive sense of well-being. Imbalance in one or more quadrants can cause symptoms of illness. Addressing issues of imbalance can potentially diminish negative symptoms and enrich our quality of life.

The use of the medicine wheel in this way is an example of holistic practice. I discovered this notion while in a counseling group and realized my own life was very much out of balance. When we come to view our lives as represented by this wheel and understand that our physical, mental, emotional, and spiritual well-being requirements all need to be in balance for us to function well, we experience growth.

In addition, a person's healing requires the individual to *transcend* the ego rather than strengthen it, as Western counseling aims to do.

In addition to these teachings and traditions of my aboriginal background, I've come to know and practice the seven sacred grandmother/grandfather teachings and principles of the Anishinaabe people, who are my ancestors. These guiding principles are necessary for our cultural foundation and include the following:

- truth as it pertains to the authenticity of your own beliefs, opinions, and convictions based on moral and ethical principles
- respect or reverence for yourself and others
- humility, modesty, or humbleness beyond meekness and pretentiousness
- courage and bravery to go beyond your comfort zone when necessary
- wisdom and knowledge to understand and contribute to other perspectives and viewpoints
- honesty or trustworthiness, so that others may depend on you and your commitments and promises
- love that includes your ability to have acceptance, empathy, understanding, and compassion for yourself and others that at times requires forgiveness

These guiding principles are necessary for our social foundation. The teachings of the medicine wheel and guiding principles create a biopsychosocial and spiritual foundation for human behavior and interaction. We are all one on the planes of existence that affect our physical behaviors, mental thoughts, feelings, and spiritual beliefs.

My sacred journey in life has proven to make me a stronger, more grateful person who is continuously learning to show love and have compassion for myself and others. In order to do this, one has to be compassionate and loving toward oneself first. I've always known this, but it hasn't been easy when my self-image is diminished for the sake of building up others. I have always felt guilty and selfish for practicing self-love, only to realize that this was a result of humility and modesty brought on by my own meekness.

With all the roles I have had in life, as a mother, wife, employee, sister, daughter, and friend. Getting hung up on life, being so busy as a caregiver, running errands, and with demands of others. It has made it difficult at times to practice self-care and self-love. After many years of counseling and introspection, I now love myself more than ever, and I take time for my physical and spiritual needs.

Like millions of people in North America, I've been dealing with mental health issues such as addictions, depression, and low self-esteem, which I believe have led to the debilitating chronic conditions of fibromyalgia and chronic fatigue syndrome. Growing up in a prosperity-deficient family with not the healthiest of habits was not the most enlightening or positive experience. If you love drama, I've had it all. But even through all the chaos, there was love in our hearts, and we learned to forgive one another despite our shortcomings.

As I've come to recognize the following, through my awareness of my reactions and those of others and as is affirmed by Louise Hay in her affirmation cards:

> Resentment, criticism, guilt and fear come from blaming others and not taking responsibility for your own experiences.

> The past is over and done and has no power over me. I can begin to be free in this moment. Today's thoughts create my future. I am in charge. I now take my own power back. I am safe and I am free to be me.

CHAPTER 1

My Chosen Family of Origin and the Dramas It Fostered

"Don't Take Anything Personally—Nothing others do is because of you. What others say and do is a projection of their own reality, their own dreams. When you are immune to the opinions and actions of others, you won't be the victim of needless suffering."

Don Miguel Ruiz – The Four Agreements

Finding balance in one's life is not an easy feat. While I was working and bringing up my family, I struggled with the work/life/family balance. I felt guilty for wanting to be with my family more, but I also loved my career and needed it for more reasons than the money. It was my life, and so was my family.

As I read Dr. Wayne Dyer's *Being in Balance*, it occurred to me that I still struggle with balance in my life, although my needs are a little different these days. We still all have choices to make; after all, we are only human. However, by reading and applying his principles, I am finally feeling more in balance day by day. As he's made me aware, "balancing how you see yourself with what you project to the world" is not an easy task. And the words that really resonated with me follow:

> Practice giving peace away wherever you go by imagining that only thoughts of peace are in the container within you. Offer these energies wherever possible. Become a peacemaker with your fellow workers, your family members, and especially those with whom you're in a love relationship. Leave your ego outside, where it can't extinguish your candle flame. Then offer someone with whom you usually argue and make wrong, a new thought from the light:
>
> *You're making a good point; I'll think about that or thanks for giving your opinion; I value what you have to say.*

These statements may shock a person at first, but you know that you're practicing becoming a being of peace by giving away what doesn't matter.

> I care not what others think of what I do, but I care very much about what I think of what I do. That is Character!
>
> —Theodore Roosevelt

It is better to be hated for what you are, than loved for
what you are not.

—Andre Gide

We are all entitled to our opinions and shouldn't be made to feel
less than or belittled for having an opposing view. I learned how to set
boundaries when I wasn't in agreement with someone's way of living
or with their views on life. It took me only forty years or so to know
the difference between what was mine and what was theirs. I also had
to make peace with those in my life who wanted me to conform to
their realities. I had to learn to set boundaries.

No matter how much my family tried to convince me that living
an impoverished existence was our lot in life, I refused to buy into
it and believed in better and greater things to manifest. And though
I love them with all my heart, I could not accept that a mediocre
lifestyle was meant for me. I just want to ask for loving kindness from
those of my clan who are still living or will be with me from the other
side. I enjoy their presence from the spiritual realm, and I assure you
they understand where I'm coming from and can relate. Living a
complacent lifestyle was not for me.

My first realization that I had a shattered ego and soul connection
was when I began to have emotional breakdowns in early childhood.
They only got worse in my late teens and early twenties. The
dysfunctional environment I found myself in at the time was not
very healthy or emotionally supportive. Due to my low self-image and
lack of understanding of my own significance, I did not know how
to fit in or be in a relationship. I didn't know enough about what a
healthy relationship with family and friends or romantic partners was
supposed to look like and feel like. But I knew I wanted to be loved,
so I continued to love and make peace the best I knew how.

I've come to know that love is a choice, and we always have it in us
to give. I knew I had it in my heart to be loving and tried my hardest
to be perceived as joyful, playful, loving, helpful, caring, thoughtful,
and compassionate toward others. After all, it's in our nature to
want to give and receive all these emotions and to feel connected

3

to one another. However, I was not allowed to express my emotions, especially if they were negative or desirous of better things. I had blockages in my mental, emotional, and spiritual consciousness that prevented me from being the person I truly wanted to be—someone who projected love, kindness, and a nonjudgmental attitude.

These types of emotions did not always serve me well in my darkest hours and in some situations where I needed to protect myself psychically. I've always been a highly sensitive person; I've come to identify myself as an empath. I was very receptive to people's feelings and the vibes of my surroundings. I learned how to tune into or tune out of most unpleasant situations in my environment. However, I was still being influenced and programmed by my family of origin, who taught me a few of life's soul lessons.

As one of the many wise spiritual teachers on my sacred journey, Sara Wiseman, explained, I've recently learned the effects of family karma. From the course "Release Yourself from Family Karma," most families must deal with:

> The thing to remember is that almost every family has dysfunction. This could be in the form of really big issues such as abuse of any kind—physical, sexual, emotional. Unfortunately, this is really common. But there's also everyday drama—maybe we don't get along, we fight or disagree, or we carry old grudges. All of this—the hurts, wounds, drama, and dysfunction— are issues we're asked to work through as soul lessons.

When I was young, I believe my oldest brother had a profound influence on how I viewed myself and the world at large. I thought of him as an atheist and gothic, as he was quite the psychedelic and medieval artist back in the day, with his portrayals of dragons, demons, and scantily clad goddesses adorning his room and other areas of our home. Most of these images terrified me and made me believe in the underworld. He had quite the influence on my belief in the darkness of the world and other unworldly portals. And although

I wasn't in alignment with his beliefs and way of living, I knew he cared about me and tried his hardest to protect me in more ways than I welcomed.

He reminded me of a warrior at times. His obsession over my safety only pushed me away from him because I was afraid, he would hurt or scare away those I wanted to be close to. He also insisted on being the protector of our household and ensured we were all safe in the best way he knew how. But at the same time, his tough persona and view of the world only added to the drama and instability in our lives.

In fact, most people in my family and our neighborhood were programmed to believe and to wear a tough persona as that's what we were all viewed by outsiders. We were the tough guys, so no one would mess with us.

My brother often discouraged me to see my attractiveness as an advantageous commodity unlike most of my other relatives had. And like most women, I was surely being influenced by my worth as a woman, compared to the portrayal of women's beauty depicted in magazines, television, and throughout our homes.

I know better now. I should not care or compare myself to others. But back then, I was surrounded primarily by men who adored and discussed other women's assets. It sometimes made me feel uncomfortable, but I loved hanging out with the guys, that included my brothers, uncles, and their friends—the ones who respected me, that is.

As Don Miguel Ruiz, author of *The Four Agreements*, advises:

> Don't Take Anything Personally—Nothing others do is because of you. What others say and do is a projection of their own reality, their own dreams. When you are immune to the opinions and actions of others, you won't be the victim of needless suffering.

I appreciated my brother for believing that I was intelligent enough to make something of myself other than becoming a model, beauty queen, or hooker. However, back then, I had a secret yearning to be a model or beauty pageant queen, as my aunt used to encourage me whenever she was around, advising me to pursue these goals. She also loved dressing me up with makeup and taking me out to places that, at my age, I should have never been in. I loved the attention she and my uncles gave me though, as my mom did not believe in this type of encouragement because she thought it would make me conceited or vain.

On the one hand, my brother was against enhancing one's attractiveness, but on the other, he esteemed women by painting them as goddesses and admiring women who were being demeaned in porn magazines, movies, and posters. I'm sure it was my own jealousy and low self-esteem, but I really resented these portrayals of women and the porn in our home. In fact, I made it a mission to destroy any such magazines or movies that I came across, to protect those of us who I felt were being victimized by it.

I believe that due to the early exposure to porn and other demoralizing depictions of women in our home, my three other brothers (who are now deceased) were obsessed with sexual muses that, in my opinion and in those of others, bordered on pedophilia and sex addiction. This may have been a karmic trait or shadow passed down from generations on both my mother's and father's sides of the family.

This is one of the family shadows that neither of my parents could face or deal with in a constructive manner. Back then, there was no counseling available for this mental disorder, and my parents truly believed it was a phase my brothers would grow out of. Even when I confided in them about it, they refused to believe it was "that bad" and considered it as "just a growing phase." They would try to convince me that women's bodies were a thing of beauty, and it was natural for us to flaunt. This just never resonated with me.

Despite me and my now-deceased sister's constant complaints, it seemed nothing was ever done about it. Unfortunately, I believe my sister was victimized more than I, as I was able to defend myself by being assertive and hostile toward their disrespect. I threatened to tell my oldest brother, who despised this type of behavior, and an uncle who was also extremely obsessed with protecting us and had a violent temper. I believed either of them would have hurt them badly. Despite the lurking and disrespectful advances, I could not get myself to tell, for fear of the repercussions. All in all, I grew up distrusting them and most people and did not sleep well in my surroundings. However, I do love and forgive them for their trespasses and hope their souls have grown on the other side.

My younger sister, I later found out, endured more, and what happened to her by one of my brothers wasn't morally right. I tried to stop it to no avail and felt so powerless and sorry for her. He came across as such a caring individual, and I couldn't understand why he tormented her.

Later in life, when she managed to forgive my brothers, she allowed the other one back into her life and found out he molested yet another innocent and helpless minor. She later charged him, and he spent a year in jail. Although I loved my brother, I could not allow him into my life, as he admitted to me that he had a problem and wouldn't be able to change. I was determined to prevent any of this in my own daughters' lives and so cut all ties with him.

Even though I loved my brothers and forgave them for their trespasses, living with them was sometimes dreadful. I resented being female because of it and sometimes wished that I was a male instead. Not only did I have to deal with them, but I also had to put up with derogatory comments and sexual advances from other male guests and strangers who believed that I was a sex figure to be toyed with.

I unfortunately developed into a woman very early in life and had a figure and curves that I was not so proud of; it felt more like a curse. I was a tomboy and wanted to hang out with the boys. Most times, I was teased and taunted by almost every male I encountered at home, at school, at friends' homes, and while walking on the street. As one of my uncles put it, I was built like a brick house and stuck out like a sore thumb. Still not sure if this was a put-down or a compliment; however, I took it as being unique, as we all are.

All in all, I knew I was attractive; I just didn't have the confidence to be the woman that I strived to be, which was more like Wonder Woman or one of Charlie's Angels from back in the day. I admired these women and found solace in watching these types of sitcoms. However, the closest I got to be a beauty queen was when I was chosen as the freshie queen in my junior high school year, which was a humbling and absolving feat. I was so shy and uncomfortable at having this type of attention directed to me. But it was very exciting, and I was so honored to have been chosen. I felt empowered, and it released some of the bondage of my self-consciousness of being a beautiful and confident woman.

Although I was able to divert undesirable attention away from myself in a friendly and assertive manner most times, there were times I had to flee or fight to save my dignity. Unfortunately, there were times when I was taken advantage of, especially after drinking too much alcohol or being under the influence of drugs, and I had to live with the shame and guilt that followed. I believe that these incidences of unwelcome sexual attention contributed to me not being able to find the healthy relationships and intimacy I so wanted in my late teen and adult years. It seemed that I was either being victimized by the men in my life or being begrudged by the women in my life, who I wanted friendships with. I felt cursed for my physical appearance and sexuality.

I didn't always believe that I was an attractive, intelligent, and creative woman. And as an introvert with low self-esteem, it took effort to be congenial. I tried hard to be friendly and outgoing and found not so healthy ways to open up, as I was extremely shy. I guess all the attention I was getting or not getting was meant to help me come out of my shell, which felt more like a hell hole I was in. All I wanted was to have real friends and healthy relationships that didn't involve sex, drugs, and alcohol.

I didn't find it comfortable to be in this sex-obsessed world, and I became very angry and depressed. I isolated myself to avoid being dragged into it. I just didn't want to be a part of this way of life. I felt that I didn't fit in unless I partook in the acceptance of porn, drugs, alcohol, and violence that were so freely available and normalized in our society. I knew and felt from deep within my soul's calling that there was a better, moral life out there. I had to live in faith and believe that it would find me if only I stayed true to myself.

I used to think, who am I to question or go against these beliefs that people around me are holding to by idolizing women's beauty and accepting the vices to cope with life? Why is there so much emphasis and passion put into displays that are meant to arouse our curiosity for a commodity that is intended to soothe our needs and desires? Is it only me who can see through the lies that people make to hook us into believing we need to be that way and accept it in order to be happy?

Growing up in an environment with a myriad of addicts to sex, drugs, alcohol, and whatever vice was available, I did whatever it took to survive and escape the power of those in charge. It appeared that the media and society and those buying into these unhealthy vices, were obsessed and brainwashed to believe in unattainable perfectionism. It appeared society's goal was to manipulate, manage, and control all aspects of our lives.

Asking for and accepting help was another unfamiliar pattern because so much energy had been invested in looking good and acting as if everything was fine when it wasn't.

I did what many adult children of addicts do; I fled, trying to create my own life but unconsciously recreating all the dynamics and dramas of my family of origin. I had no awareness of my feelings or other aspects of normal development and ended up with friends and partners who were also addicted to the dramas of survival.

CHAPTER 2

Shifting Outlooks Despite the Diagnosis

"I help create a world where it is safe to love each other –
Every time I meditate or do a visualization or healing, I am
connecting with like-minded people all over the planet."

Power Thought Cards – Louise Hay

When I was fifteen, I didn't want to be part of planet Earth any longer and contemplated taking my life. One day, after being grounded for some reason that I cannot recall, I decided to take a handful of prescription pills. I had no idea what they were.

At the time, we were living in a subsidized housing complex in a low-income neighborhood known as Little Chicago. Besides my mom, my six siblings, my aunt, her husband, and their children, we also had another family of four living with us in a four-bedroom townhouse. I'm not sure where everyone else slept, but I did have a room with my sister, and I tried to keep it neat enough to be our sanctuary.

Living with all those people wasn't always comfortable. I usually wanted to be away from them, and I did whenever possible, stayed over at friends' or other relatives.

The people living with us were a nice family though, who needed to move here from another province for some reason that I believe had to do with a marriage breakdown. As I recall, there were two sisters, who were friends of my mom, and their children, one daughter and two sons. They were kind of cool, and I really liked them.

On top of being violated and mistreated by my immediate family and other people brought around by my relatives. My mother's immediate family would drop in frequently they wanted and would hang out, eat, drink, chain-smoke, and, to me, overstay their welcome. I didn't take well to all of the hustle and bustle and felt so imprisoned and agitated that I was at the end of my rope. I didn't have any hope or desire for the future.

To my amazement, one of the guys staying with us, who reminds of Archangel Michael, noticed how agitated and high I was and offered me some coffee. I had never tried coffee prior to that, but I think it saved my life. I was going through some awful hallucinations and was frightened and trembling. I believe that my spirit guides and angels were working overtime that day to save me, as I sure felt their presence. It was intense.

I recently received a message from Archangel Michael from Doreen Virtue's angel guidance app that I have on my phone. It reminded me so much of this situation that I must include it in this story: "Pray, God please heal my heart, and feel yourself uplifted by God's loving angels." I believe this is what I was praying for that day.

After that episode of desperation and awakening, I decided that maybe life wasn't so bad after all and tried to live a healthier lifestyle. I started reading and studying self-help books while trying to find my spiritual higher self that most religious figures were referring to. This would be the beginning of my sacred journey—however rocky and clammy it was to meander through.

When I was in my early twenties, I decided to seek professional counseling. I found that mainstream psychologists were not very helpful and couldn't provide the help I was seeking. Looking back, I was seeking validation of my connection to the divine source of our creator and my higher self. However, due to life's callings and the business of life, I got sidetracked by responsibilities of work and family, which left too little time for self-reflection and self-care. I began to search and do research in my spare time. I needed to know why I felt so down and miserable about life and why I felt the emptiness within me.

Later in life, I was diagnosed with depression and fibromyalgia and used drugs and alcohol to numb my emotional and physical pains. Although calming, I found them to be very toxic, and they didn't help me feel normal or empowered. Although I still use them occasionally, I hope to someday find better coping mechanisms to overcome their stronghold on my being. I know I can't continue to abuse my body in this way. I live in the hope that there is a better way, and I strive to find healthy ways to cope.

Despite my vices, I do believe in using natural alternative medicines or home remedies for mental health and other aches and pains and minor illnesses. There is so much available on alternative medicine, out there these days. And the studies being done for their effectiveness are improving.

As mentioned, I've been on a roller-coaster ride of self-improvement from my teens and have been practicing alternative medicines with herbs and supplements for as long as I can remember. I am truly grateful for all the naturalists who have written books on health and wellness. I have also had opportunities to take workshops on healing modalities such as quantum touch, Reiki, tapping, integrated energy therapy, and angel and crystal therapy, and I continue to study these energy healing/touch treatments.

In addition to these energy-healing modalities, I have also been using alternative healing practices, such as going to a chiropractor, reflexologist, acupuncturist, and massage therapist. I've been relying on these modalities since I was in my early twenties and have always found them to be quite beneficial and supportive of my healing. I am also studying chair massage and reflexology with the intention of working on and guiding others to better health and wellbeing

I started seeing a chiropractor in my late teens due to a back problem that resulted from an injury sustained from falling off a horse and landing on my hip.

I was horseback riding with friends out at a ranch in the Interlake area. I loved horses and loved being out in the country. My brother-in-law at the time was working for a horse ranch as a trail ride master and offered to take us out on the trails. I was given a beautiful but feisty horse to ride. She loved to gallop and run. After about an hour or two of riding, we were heading back to the stables full speed, and suddenly I went flying off the horse, saddle and all. For some reason, the saddle was not secured properly and let loose. Luckily, I fell between two trees, or things could have been worse. I fractured my hip but for some reason never made it to the ER. I was in pain and limping for a few days but amazed that it healed, or so I thought.

A few years later while pregnant and after having my son, I began to experience excruciating lower back pain. But, instead of taking drugs for the pain, I went to a chiropractor, and he helped make it better for a while.

A few years after that, I was working with this wonderful lady. Her name was Joan, and I am forever grateful she hired me for my first real job as a computer operator/ accounts receivable clerk. When I mentioned my pain symptoms to her, she advised me to see this reflexologist she knew. He was also a physiotherapist and a naturopath. I was amazed that not only did he work on my feet and hands, which I loved, he also worked on my back. When I told him my symptoms, he measured my spine and hip alignment and noticed that my hips were out by at least two inches. After the reflexology, he would push my hip into place ever so gently. After about three visits, I was so relieved and felt better than ever. This is when I really started to believe in alternative medicine.

And because of my episode with pharmaceuticals, I became extremely sensitive to any type of drug, including any typical over the counter (OTC) pain reliever, and couldn't take them for pain. I began to rely on home remedies and alternative medicines and was never convinced that pharmaceuticals were the answer to our health problems. I am hoping that I will never become majorly ill and have to depend on them. I've seen the effects they can have on our bodies. Reading about and studying the side effects of some drugs is enough to scare most individuals, including me, away from them.

Prior to visiting with your physician, it is helpful to study your disorder on the web or at your local library. Try to find any natural remedy or supplements you and your doctor might consider. I suggest this, as most physicians will not recommend natural alternatives unless requested to do so. As a result, I have been taking various supplements for all my diagnosed ailments with success.

With our biopsychosocial makeup, practicing alternative therapies while applying energy-healing techniques is now conventional. Over the years, alternative medicines and practices have been proven to be beneficial in more ways than one for me and my family. I've been accustomed to diagnosing and providing healing to my family's health care needs and am so blessed that we've all been healthy, besides the occasional spiritual breakdowns. After all, taking care of our health and wellness is our responsibility and I am determined to practice and teach others how to accomplish this.

I know there are times when a person can become very sick and be diagnosed with a major illness or virus that may require a more sophisticated medicine to help them heal. Most drugs or OTC medicines available are approved by the Federal Drug Administration and other health care bodies but do not necessarily have to be, such as naturopathic medicine, herbs, and supplements. So, again, patient research is necessary, and one must consider the pros and cons for the benefits and side effects that may be experienced. I believe most people are intuitive and can decide what is best for their own wellbeing.

I foresee that most of my readers are those people who may be suffering in silence and need hope for what lies ahead and encouragement to step into the sacred place of wellbeing. They may have gone through life being abused and bullied by addicts or power seekers and have had to swallow their pride at times to be nice or for safety reasons. I hope to give you some tools to use to combat your own ailments and provide a road map for self-healing and wellness.

Most of us want to get along with other people and be at peace within our world. We don't need the negative drama and commotion in our life, but our ego believes otherwise. Most of us want a normal life, whatever our egoic definition of normal is. Mostly, we want a life where we can be ourselves and make new discoveries about ourselves and our environment. We want to be fulfilled and happy and experience the joy that we all deserve and strive for.

However, there are those who don't know any better and may feel a need to have drama in their lives. They will create it by gossip, speculation, and assumptions of others and events by trying to convince us that their opinions are right. I refer to these people as the drama kings and queens who find it necessary to have episodes of chaos or excitement in their daily living. I know I did at certain times and to this day find it difficult to avoid.

I'm convinced this is another by-product of living in dysfunction and chaos and the illusion of an amorous life. Add to that the allure of glamour and drama portrayed on television soap operas and other dramatic sitcoms and movies, most of which I loved watching. I admit, growing up I was addicted to the soaps and sitcoms on television. With all the adventure, glamour, beauty and richness of the rich and famous. And of course, in almost every scene, people were shooting back a cocktail and dressed impeccably. I wanted to be like them and have the glamorous life they had. I thought that the more drama and material possessions I had in my life, the closer to this lifestyle I was, and my mediocre life would be enhanced.

What I saw and experienced added to this was the borderline porno displayed in advertisements, movies, and music videos. Showing such an exaggerated portrayal of romanticism and eroticism of life.

Our innocent young minds are presented with this throughout our lives. It's no wonder that we are all psychologically messed up. We are in search of an unattainable validation of our worth as an average human being by pursuing this type of reality.

Being exposed to the sex, violence and unhealthy behaviors on dramatic TV shows and movies created a PTSR or post-traumatic stress reaction in me, as Doreen Virtue explains in her book *Don't Let Anything Dull Your Sparkle*. This hypervigilance made me feel uneasy and terrified after watching a frightful or horrific movie, to the point of becoming anxious and agitated and not being able to sleep or I'd have nightmares.

I realized this early on in life and so avoided movie nights with friends and family, unless of course it was suggested that we watch a chick flick or comedy, as these were the only kind of movies I could tolerate. I enjoy some drama if there isn't a lot of gore and guts involved. I am cognizant and emotionally affected by any situation that causes drama or trauma, such as emotional or physical pain. I am aware of my own post-traumatic stress reaction, and I am cognizant of the intense fear and helplessness that has occurred in my own life.

I used to think—and I'm sure others did as well—that I was a victim or miss prudish because I was not into all the action-packed drama in movies. And as a highly sensitive empath, I've always been very saddened by the horror, violence, and crimes depicted in movies and video games. I have never had much tolerance or acceptance for this overdramatization and cruelty to humankind, and less so these days.

I no longer watch videos that show drama and violence and try to limit my intake of overromanticized shows. I do, however, enjoy the not so violent sitcoms on the air today and can tolerate some crime shows; if the perpetrator is apprehended, I am at peace. I even might watch something frightful if there is some comedy or wonderment added to it, such as a science fiction, alien, or fiend show.

I've always known (and am so relieved that spiritual teachers agree). That even watching these types of smut (as it was called in my home) on television or in movies can have a traumatic effect on us. It is also known that what you think is what you'll become. Therefore, I do not want to be like or have these characters in my life any longer.

Of course, some of us want to be the good guy, the hero, the one who brings justice and fairness into our world of imbalance and chaos. I am so glad to have a partner who also agrees that the world does not need more violence, tragedy, and vindictiveness shown on television but could use more shows that portray love, kindness, and compassion.

CHAPTER 3

Insight into My Health Challenges

"I can heal myself on all Levels – Healing means
to make whole and to accept all parts of myself –
not just the parts I like, but all of me."

Power Thought Cards – Louise Hay

As stated, from Doreen Virtue's audiobook *Don't Let Anything Dull Your Sparkle*. Sometimes, unknowingly being exposed to trauma resulting from mistreatment or physical, emotional, and mental abuse can cause post-traumatic stress disorder that can bring on psychological effects such as being anxious, also known as anxious stress syndrome or dissociation. These were some of the health challenges I had to deal with.

Most health challenges are the result of emotional turmoil and other trials we humans face along our journey of life, that we do not become aware of until later, when we are able to step back and reminisce without judgment or attachment. In this book, I would like to share how my experiences with tragic events, trauma, and addictions have contributed to the dis-eases in my life—and I'm sure in others that have known suffering. However, I do not want to or intend to recreate them, so as not to cause further trauma. I also believe and was informed, just talking about one's traumatic experiences can do this.

It is the synchronicities of our divinely led path I want to tell you about. I've been led down a spiritual path to help me heal or, if I may rephrase, deal with life's ups and downs. I would like to give thanks to my spiritual teachers, primarily from Hay House and other spiritual groups. Their wisdom and teachings have contributed to my health and well-being and new outlook on life. You see, being able to cope with this illness they call fibromyalgia (fibro) is not an easy task. As anyone can attest to, it's not easy to consistently be in a positive mind-set with an open heart, as we are all counselled to do by our spiritual guides and teachers.

Although I know and feel the effects of my illness, I choose not to let it define me. So instead of complaining about how I am experiencing its effects on me, I choose to use excerpts from our health experts to describe its effects on the masses overall.

What is fibro?

It is identified as a disorder known to cause muscle
and joint aches and pain all over the body. It is a

chronic ongoing condition of pain, stiffness and constant fatigue. The condition affects millions of people and is usually diagnosed in middle age, although symptoms may start at an earlier age. It primarily occurs in women, but men and children can contract it as well, as is the case with my sibling. As defined by the WRHA in Canada.

How does it arise?

What causes fibromyalgia is not scientifically known. But the condition has been linked to: As defined by the WRHA in Canada.

- Emotional or physical stress or distress,
- Anxiety resulting in lack of restful sleep and being on edge,
- Depression and other mental health issues,
- Addictions to substances meant to alleviate the symptoms,
- Post Traumatic Stress Disorders (PTSD) - events such as a car accident or other traumatic event,
- Being bullied or physically and emotionally abused,
- Infections or other illness.

I've seen its effects on many others, including most of my family members, especially the depression and desperation for relief. Witnessing, hearing, and feeling their emotional state growing up was unsettling, as their outbursts of irritation and chronic self-loathing were not easy to live with. Their coping mechanisms did not resonate with me either. Not only were pharmaceuticals and alcohol the go-to remedy to block the pain, various other substances were being used as medication to numb their discomfort. However, their health did not seem to improve, and it appeared that nothing was being done on a physical or emotional level to alleviate their pain and suffering.

Mind you, my oldest brother did have a few major accidents in his lifetime. Being burned badly in our house fire when he was a teen, was only the beginning for him. I was around four or five at the time. I woke up and saw flames with smoke coming from the dining room. Luckily, I was sleeping next to my dad at the time and woke him up. He quickly scooped up my sister and me, and we all sat in the vehicle, watching the colorful flames and firemen dousing them.

I'm not sure about all the details, but I guess the firemen pulled my brother from the kitchen where the fire started and took him to a hospital. He had severe burns. Luckily, three of my brothers were at camp and didn't need rescuing.

Because my older brother didn't drive or own a vehicle and rode a bicycle wherever he needed to go, he endured major injuries from being struck various times by vehicles while riding on the street. He was in a coma twice because of these injuries and is now on permanent disability. Today he is coping with the aid of painkillers and cannabis.

I am only now realizing that the dramas and traumas we endure while experiencing life can contribute to a person's needy ways. To this day, my brother never ceases to remind me about times in my life where he supposedly saved me from a bully. Despite the fact I didn't need saving, I am grateful for him and what he has done for me and especially for our family. I really appreciate him today for taking care of my aging mother and doing his best to take care of our townhouse.

I do not know the entire story of my other siblings and relatives, but for whatever reasons that I did not understand at the time, they were convinced they had a condition that required medical intervention. I've noticed that some of them displayed hypochondriac tendencies and ran to a medical doctor often, looking for some kind of fix (narcotic or drug) for their ailments. So, it became the norm; I was programmed to believe that doctors and drugs could cure any ailment that was bothering me, no matter how minor it was.

I too fell into this neurotic state of relying on the medical field to fix my mostly mental and emotional problems that emerged as physical. All in all, I believe I am doing well physically, besides the occasional flare-ups of the fibro and seasonal affective disorder

(SAD), where I become sad and achy for a few days or weeks at a time during damp or cold weather changes.

SAD is a type of depression that's related to changes in seasons. SAD begins and ends at about the same time every year. If you're like most people with SAD, your symptoms start in the fall and continue into the winter months, sapping your energy and making you feel moody.

I don't want to sound cynical, as I do believe there are some physicians who have our best interests at heart. But I don't completely have faith in all the pharmaceutical interventions, especially with all the side effects. I have always been very sensitive to drugs and will, under doctors' orders, try certain drugs until the side effects become intolerable. I find it appalling that even with all the researched and transparent side effects for certain medications people still put their trust in them.

After many years of anguish and seeking medical attention for depression, PMS, chronic fatigue, headaches, achiness, and anxiety, I had to find a way to deal with the pain and discomfort I was experiencing. There were many times when I was encouraged to try pharmaceutical drugs to assist with my physical discomforts and emotional pain. However, my main hope was to find more holistic alternatives for my health and well being.

I have had a few very good physicians in my life and one physician who took me seriously and referred me to a neuro specialist. The physician was so understanding and helpful. He was very personable, and I will always be grateful to him for his concern for me. Unfortunately, he decided to transfer to another province.

The neuro specialist tested my nerves and muscles, and after noticing that my pain threshold to being touched was not good, he determined that I had fibro.

While going through all my PMS symptoms and being diagnosed with fibroids and then perimenopause and other health struggles was no picnic for me and my family, I believe I did okay.

I would have welcomed the teachings of Christiane Northrup, whose books I have recently read and whose audios I listened to regarding *Creating Physical and Emotional Health During the Change.*

As well as another book called *Women's Bodies, Women's Wisdom and the Wisdom of Menopause* has been very helpful in coming to terms with my symptoms.

Also, Lissa Rankin, MD, author of *Write Your Own Prescription,* is a very wise intuitive medical physician with wonderful advice.

They both remind me of a very optimistic physician I once had who was so cheerful and positive about life. I loved visiting with her for her positive disposition of life. Whenever I would go to her for an ailment, I would forget why I was there.

I have also done my own diagnosing and practiced alternative medicines and holistic healing systems prior to visiting my doctor for most of my life. Together we would find the least intrusive remedy that would not harm my body in other ways with side effects.

In Doreen Virtue's book *Assertiveness for Earth Angels,* she explains what a "light worker" is. Some of us "Earth Angels are sometimes called Lightworkers, and the two terms are fairly interchangeable." I believe some of us, including physicians, are earth angels, and our gift is to heal.

As earth angels, we are here to work under God's direction. Therefore, I have been summoned to be a light worker and healer of self and others. I believe our purpose here is to be of service to one another by displaying acts of love and kindness. I am ready for his assignments to serve others and to enjoy this wonderous and at times turbulent life on this earthly plane. I truly believe that we deserve to have a joyous, healthy, and prosperous life, free of drama and suffering.

CHAPTER 4

My Early Days on This Earthly Plane

"I am centered in truth and peace. I search my heart for injustices I still harbor. I forgive them and let them go."

Wisdom Cards - Louise Hay

Because my visionary way of thinking was not the norm in my family, I was always labeled snobbish and had to deal with envious and discourteous backlash for most of my growing years. Yes, jealousy is one of the unspoken shadows of our family karma of dysfunction, a trait I had to work on to defeat. Yet, whatever my mind-set was to rise above my circumstances at the time, I am still being influenced and taunted by my immediate family and friends. I resolved that it is just the karma that we must deal with.

One of my spiritual advisors, Sara Wiseman, explains family karma (or shadows) that we must deal with and cannot hide from. As previously stated in chapter 1:

> The thing to remember is that almost every family has dysfunction ...
>
> When we first leave home, typically in early adulthood or younger, we have this sense of freedom-we can leave all those problems and never come back. But as we become adults, we find that you can leave geographically, you can even stop all contact, but the emotional and energetic residue of issues left unresolved will eventually have to be worked out. Our inner work-our soul work-is what creates our healing. There are lots of ways to heal-you can go to therapy or read books or take workshops or join support groups. The approach of this work is spiritual, which means we work through issues from the soul perspective.

This resonated so much with me that I signed up for this short course called "Releasing Yourself from Family Karma." I believed it would help me heal my emotional wounds. Yes, after studying this course and reading numerous self-help books, going to individual therapy, and attending workshops and group counselling sessions, I came to realize that I had lessons to learn from all my current and past relationships. It only took the last forty years or so to have this epiphany, but as advised, it is never too late to change your story.

I already knew I had to deal with the inner struggles of being overly sensitive to the negative energies surrounding me and within me. While trying to appear strong and capable on the outside. What didn't make things easy was that, I noticed that not only my family of origin but also the people I chose to be in my life were not in alignment with their higher selves and had family karma and other dependence issues to deal with.

On an encouraging note, there were some admirable families and individuals that I crossed paths with that influenced my sphere of illumination and enlightenment. I am truly thankful for them and have acknowledged them in this story of my life. I once read this by an unknown author, and is so true for me:

> People Come into Your Path for a Reason, a Season or a Lifetime:
> When someone is in your life for a REASON:
>
> - It is usually to meet a need you have expressed.
> - They have come to assist you through a difficulty.
> - To provide you with guidance and support.
> - To aid you physically, emotionally or spiritually.
> - They may seem like they are a godsend, and they are.
> - They are there for the reason you need them to be.
> - Then without any wrongdoing on your part, or at an inconvenient time, this person will say or do something to bring the relationship to an end.
> - Sometimes they die, sometimes they walk away.
> - Sometimes they act up and force you to take a stand.
>
> What we must realize is that our need has been met, our desire fulfilled. Their work is done. The prayer

you sent up has now been answered and now it is time to move on.

Some people come into your life for a SEASON:

- Because your turn has come to share, grow or learn.
- They bring you an experience of peace or make you laugh.
- They may teach you something you have never done.
- They usually give you an unbelievable amount of joy.
- Believe it, it is real. But only for a season.

LIFETIME relationships teach you lifetime lessons:

- Things you must build upon to have a solid emotional foundation.
- Your job is to accept the lesson, love the person, and put what you have learned to use in all other relationships and areas of your life.
- It is said that love is blind, but friendship is clairvoyant.
- Thank you for being a part of my life. - Whether you were a reason, a season or a lifetime.

—Unknown author

I've wholeheartedly embraced the teachings of those people who have come into my life for whatever reason, season, or lifetime, including my earth angels, ancestors, and spiritual advisors, and I've absorbed their lessons. There is so much that I learned from and witnessed in these people who helped guide me through the perils of living in a constructive manner.

I've learned that tragedies and traumas may not be blessings, but blessings and lessons can come out of them. I am learning to overcome life's challenges and lessons through constant self-realization and focusing on who I really am meant to be. By practicing and living authentically I will strive for wellness. I have been given divine signals that I am more. I am a divine being of energy who is here to experience the greater life that I've always longed for. I will operate under God's guidance beyond the veil of illusion that a traditional life portrays. I am ready to serve others on their path to health and wellness by encouraging their own spiritual growth and intuitive knowledge. You may find more information at my website at Yourdivineinspirations.com.

CHAPTER 5

Becoming Aware of My Compulsions and Need for Self-Discovery

"I see my patterns and I choose to make changes"
Louise Hay – Affirmation Cards

"I live in the now. Each moment is new.
I choose to see my self worth. I love and approve of myself"
Heal Your Body - Louise Hay

Besides using prescribed drugs to deal with my emotional and physical pains, I soon began to use alcohol and other sugary substances to numb the pain and relax me. Even though I convinced myself and others that I did not have a problem with it, I felt the short-term and long-term effects were not very pleasant. I hated myself sometimes for overindulging and felt like crap the next day or two. I soon felt the need to surrender to my higher power, as I did not want to live my life addicted to drugs or alcohol—immobilized and miserable about life.

The following is by Ana Holub in *Heal Addictions with Forgiveness*:

> Addictions of all kinds, whether they are hard or soft, obvious or subtle, steal our life force. In order to heal, we must reclaim ourselves — our minds, hearts and bodies — and refill our inner reservoir of vitality and happiness.

> *'One thing that addiction does is, it freezes you. You don't develop, you don't learn the skills by trial and error of having experiences and learning from them, and finding out what it is you want, and how to go about getting it, by relating with other people. You short-circuit all that stuff and just go for the button that says this feels good over and over again.'* — James Taylor

> On Earth, we each play a part in an immense drama of pain, suffering, and disillusionment. In despair, we think this 3D world is all there is and of course, this belief is incredibly depressing. It's no wonder that there are so many addicts and so many kinds of addictions! But when we are ready (and not a moment before), we choose to turn around and start walking toward Spirit.

Truly, this about-face is a miracle. With spiritual
support, we crawl out of the pit we made and realize
there's a new world of serenity and sanity.

Forgiveness is the deep letting go that's essential when
you are ready to turn around.

After realizing that I had to heal and get in touch with my spiritual
side, I desired a new path, a sacred path to follow. I wanted to become
more optimistic and proactive in coping with my addictions and this
disease in a healthy way, without becoming too attached to them. I
decided to work on my inner self to recover from trauma by following
not only Ana's teachings but also the teachings of other spiritual
advisors. I believe I needed more balance in my life, and that opened
my heart to a healing journey. One part of this has to do with staying
optimistic, strong, active, and connected.

Part of it was showing me that I needed to get back to basics.
What would make me feel good, without the vices and numbing
substances? I learned that doing moderate but exhilarating exercise
is so beneficial to my body, and I strongly believe it must be fun and
enjoyable. Exercise in any form can really make you feel better, even
though it is at times exhausting. It's a great feeling of exhaustion when
you know that part of your healing and spiritual growth was spent
improving yourself (body, mind, spirit, and soul).

I like to start off the day whenever possible with an outdoor walk
or bike ride in nature. Or, when the weather is not so great, I throw
in an exercise video on walking, yoga, or Pilates. Add to that some
dance videos and a few dance lessons, and you'll be on your way to
a more blissful lifestyle.

Other fun favorites of mine to get physical activity into my
daily, mundane life include bowling, golfing, curling, bike riding,
or kayaking, all sports that have served me well but are getting a bit
more challenging.

I recently purchased a kayak and love using it on the calm lakes
in our country. It is such an exhilarating sport for the calmness it

provides when gliding across the clear blue waters and the workout it provides rowing and getting into and out of the waters.

What makes it even more challenging is that I've always had a fear of open waters. I have been terrified of lakes and rivers most of my life. This was due to an incident as a child when I fell into a water-filled manhole while running down our neighborhood back lane. I was seven or eight years old and was trying to keep up with my siblings; we were out searching for bottles and milk jugs so we could have some spending money. I recall there were at least seven of us, and we were all running from someone or something. I suspect we weren't supposed to be where we were or doing what we were doing. I was too young at the time to know or care; all I knew was that I was having fun.

I didn't notice the construction sign beside the puddle of water. I jumped into it, as any little kid will do to get a splash, and I found myself literally over my head in water and not able to get out by myself. As I was frantically trying to reach out, I thought, *Oh my God, this is not good. I'm done for.* Well, thank God, my uncle happened to turn around. He came back and pulled me out. I was so shaken but thankful for him being there. Ever since that incident, I couldn't go near any type of dark water.

I was always determined to keep up with my family and peers, no matter how much older or stronger they appeared to be. I have always been active and wanted so much to be an athlete, and although I was very good at baseball, I loved playing and participating in all outdoor activities. I didn't have the greatest athletic abilities, but I loved trying no matter what. I was always climbing, racing, or running with the crowd. I even took a few bruises and falls while trying to keep up. I loved playing outdoors, participating in sports.

In order to cope with fibro, one must also be mindful of what one puts into one's body. After all, we've been taught that eating a balanced diet according to the pyramid scale of nutrition is a precondition to good health. Turns out that following the pyramid may not be all that good for you. When one thinks of food as a needless necessity, it's not easy to maintain and create a blend of healthy foods for a tasty diet that you can enjoy.

It could be that I was brought up on eating basic foods that were not a healthy balance; I need to force myself to eat as many organic or nonorganic veggies and fibrous foods as I can muster. Having them blended in a shake makes them a bit more palatable. I still love and need my protein; after all, I am not a rabbit but a meat eater to the core. I aim for one or two days a week without meat and enjoy a steak or hamburger once in a while—with, of course, a salad on the side. We all have individual needs for nutrition and must determine what is best for us by choosing healthy nutritious food we like.

And since fibro is also considered a mental and emotionally festered illness, You need to change your mindset and do the mental/emotional work by staying positive. And doing daily affirmations (with or without the mirror) to give yourself the love and gratitude you deserve. Your soul and spirit will thank you.

I am grateful to have known other addicts in recovery and the spiritual gurus found in various books and from attending seminars and courses in person and online. In my early days, I had psychic and divine card readings that pointed me to the right path to follow. I am truly blessed and enlightened to have found them. I will acknowledge these more as I take you on my sacred journey throughout the chapters of my life.

I am so grateful to have found spiritual teachers from all walks of life who've taught me the importance of using our mind to change our attitudes about life.

All affirmations by Louise Hay and other Hay House authors have been nothing but an inspiration for me. I suggest reading and taking into your heart and conscious mind these affirmation cards:

- *Power Thought* cards by Louise Hay
- *I Can Do It* cards by Louise Hay
- *Heart Thought* cards by Louise Hay
- *Well Being* cards by Esther and Jerry Hicks
- *Life Loves You* cards by Louise Hay and Robert Holden

I suggest any oracle or tarot decks that resonates with you, or any other inspirational and spiritual guiding tool you find.

While meditating one day, I came across this message in a *Blessings & Divination* card deck that I chose while doing a workshop. It read:

The Blessing of Letting Go

Free yourself from negative entanglements by letting go of emotional ties, beliefs and outdated ways of thinking that no longer serve you. You have the power. That which you let go will transform into an endless blessing.

I know this is not always easy to do, but again, it will free you from your negative entanglements and allow you to open up to infinite possibilities.

CHAPTER 6

Coming to Grips with My True Essence

"I am here AT THE RIGHT TIME
- The work I am doing ON MYSELF IS A LIFETIME PROCESS.
It doesn't matter how much time it takes,
because I have All the Time in the World.

Heart Thought Cards – Louise Hay

Since most of us have been programmed with guilt, doubt, and uncertainty about having the life of our dreams. We are programmed to believe that we are limited in our own destination or fate in life, and we become lethargic in ways to improve it. Most people I've crossed paths with are either existing for the sake of it or so pessimistic and cynical that I wonder what it is with our existence that brings this on. How can we have so many negative people who claim to love one another and believe in God?

Because I am a seeker of knowledge and have hope for our future, I needed to learn more about our psychological and cosmic makeup. Besides reading books on psychology and human behavior, I've studied other means of validating ourselves and our planetary existence.

I've done this with the assistance of spiritual teachers and guides, angels, and intuitive and psychic readers, as well as with the help of astrology and numerology readings. These made me believe I was equipped to succeed in life no matter what my outer circumstances were. By following these, I've had to go against mainstream notions; most do not believe and are cynical, and I have at times been ridiculed. I've had to endure the mocking of those who didn't believe and embrace those who did.

I was amazed at the accuracy, and I believe that the predictions and advice given by these spiritual divination tools have given me the hope and faith I needed to believe in myself and where I was headed.

Through all I've experienced and especially with the many instances of trauma and encountering many low-vibrational beings (that I used to refer to as jerks), I know for sure that belief in the divine essence of the creator of all that is, or God, and our higher selves is the key to staying positive and having a successful life.

In addition, spiritual awakenings and alternative healing practices have given me the strength needed to endure this debilitating condition called fibro, and they have given me the strength to strive for a better life. As my numerology chart analysis advised, I can fulfill my potential completely, or I can give into the repressive religious or intellectual dogmas that I've been programmed to believe in, to exist as a smaller version of myself. While the latter has predominantly run my life, I now choose to believe in my dreams and strive for the best.

According to some authors, disease is a motion of symptoms of your body being at dis-ease. I must admit I was in a state of dis-ease and imbalance most of my life. I know it began in my childhood, having been born into a family of dysfunction, or to put it eloquently, "the family soup of bitter flavors" who had various coping mechanisms, some not so healthy. I must admit that my resentments, stubbornness, and self-righteousness have contributed to my isolation and conflict with others.

I have come to believe in coping mechanisms that were inspired by my curiosity to seek other healing paths and alternative medicines and therapies, along with my need to understand and connect with my spiritual self. Today, I try to be pharmaceutical drug–free and have stopped taking the antidepressants, sleep agents, and painkillers prescribed, other than OTC painkillers for the real bad days.

While participating in a group therapy session for dealing with the effects of abuse on my life, I came to learn what manipulation is and learned to set boundaries with others. We focused our healing on the medicine wheel, and I began to realize that I was out of balance and low on the spiritual and emotional sides of my life.

I came to realize that we can determine where we're at on our life's sacred journey and concentrate our efforts on the planes of existence we are on. After all, we must comprehend our existence as spirits having a human experience. Most of us exist on a myriad of levels or cosmic planes simultaneously. Four of the most obvious ones are as follows:

- mind—mentality (intellectual)
- physical body
- emotional
- spiritual

I think most of us sail through life focusing on the first three; at least I did, until I realized I needed to connect to a higher power, to my spiritual side. Because of my upbringing, I was programmed to believe that the Roman Catholic or Evangelical/Baptist religious doctrines were the way to spirituality.

Because I didn't understand this concept of the church doctrine, spirituality didn't evolve in me due to my insecurities and need to fit in with all others in my circle of influence. I've encountered three types of people: believers, nonbelievers, and seekers. The nonbelievers seemed to be having more fun and connections, albeit superficial. Another aspect of being human is our need to be social beings and to connect with one another. The believers seemed to have more peace and clarity and enjoyed being in groups. And the seekers, like myself, needed proof that something was out there and needed to feel that connection. I also desired emotional connection to others.

So, from early on in life, I set out to find these spiritual beings who could show me the righteous way to live. I found my way into religious circles that mostly taught that love and light are the way to be, and if you surrender to Jesus or the Holy Spirit, you will be saved and have salvation. Although the love and light part and surrendering resonated with me, I was always left wondering what it was we were all trying to be saved from.

I grew up in a neighborhood and family of nonreligious sceptics and can't recall any of them being spiritually led. Some of my immediate family did confess to being Roman Catholic, but to my understanding, their beliefs bordered more on superstitions. I was not convinced that that religion was the way to the true essence of our being here on earth. When reading the Bible and attending services at various churches, I did not find the teachings very enlightening. They left me feeling condemned and frightened for the future, as I was a sinner and an addict at the time but still needed a connection to my spiritual self.

As time went on and my self-esteem dwindled, being spiritual and reaching out was not an easy task for me, being the introvert that I was. I was extremely shy and suffered with low self-esteem and subconsciously isolated myself by putting up walls and closing off my heart to love.

After the realization that I am a divine, spiritual being who undeniably lost her innocence early in life, I knew I must rise above and be a motivation to people rather than a burden. Although I knew I wasn't responsible for others' happiness, I gave it my best to make it.

In my earlier days, I believed in numerology and horoscopes to give me daily advice on how to lead my life. As much as I wanted to believe the positive aspects of these tools, I felt a bit misled at times when it came to the not so positive aspects, so I tried not to get too attached to the predicted outcomes.

As my expression number four suggests, my approach to life and to problems is methodical and systematic. I am a creator and a doer and determined to turn my dreams into reality by manifesting my desires. I possess a highly developed sense of structure, most times. I take my obligations and those of my family quite seriously. As a result, I am reliable and responsible. Who could argue with that? It is who I am.

After many years of consulting with the readings posted in columns in newspapers or magazines and studying a few books on the subject, I found an online tool. I was so ecstatic and grateful to have found this. I could have my readings done for me on a daily, monthly, or yearly basis and delivered to my inbox. In addition to horoscopes, the site also provided card readings and numerology.

These divine tools have served me well over the years and have contributed to my success in dealing with life's ups and downs.

Even though I believe these divinity methods have helped me navigate through life, they've also helped me succeed in my endeavors thus far. I still could not share them with just anyone, as most people I knew thought I was a bit eccentric for believing in such magical things as these. Thankfully, there are people who believed in me and these magical tools as well.

My hope is that people of faith and love find ways to assist one another on our earthly plane to discover ways to share their spiritual knowledge without offense. Although I admire what the church is doing for this, I still believe there are a lot of lost souls who need encouragement and spiritual guidance on their sacred journey to become the enlightened and illuminated beings that we are meant to be.

CHAPTER 7

My Spiritual Awakenings

"Always Do Your Best

– Your best is going to change from moment to moment,
it will be different when you are healthy as opposed to
sick. Under any circumstance, simply do your best, and
you will avoid self-judgement, self-abuse and regret."

The Four Agreements – Don Miguel Ruiz

Besides the delusional time when I tried taking my own life, my first real awakening into the spiritual realm occurred after my brother took his life at the age of twenty-one. I was nineteen at the time, living with my older brother and my son while going to school. I lived in a subsidized townhome and thought life was great. It was a bit of a struggle but still wonderous.

I heard the news and was in disbelief. I had never experienced a death in my life, so it was very traumatic. I was so devastated because I loved him so much and felt so awful and guilt ridden for not being there for him. I knew he was struggling with life, as he was not living the God-given life that we are meant to have. I guess he was just too confused and depressed to realize that life has its ups and downs and is in constant change.

If only he could have known the power of the universe to make things better. I wish I could have convinced him of this sooner. But I guess it was his soul calling to return him to the kingdom on the other side. I know for sure I will be with him again someday. In fact, when I dream about him at times, it feels so real and enlightening, like we are actually visiting each other. I believe this has to do with our psychic abilities to communicate with those who've crossed over to the other side. Thank you to my brother Greg for visiting with me in my dreams, and I am looking forward to seeing you on the other side.

Once all the funeral services and grieving of this tragedy were over, life went on. I felt his presence with me wherever I went. I continued to ask for guidance whenever I felt scared or insecure in certain places. I would ask my guardian angel, which at the time I believed to be my brother, to protect me by surrounding me in a bubble of positive light. I felt so protected and at ease with whoever and wherever I was at.

I later discovered that there are guardian angels, spirit guides, and archangels who watch over us and are there for us whenever we need them. We all have them. All we need to do is ask. I'd been doing this throughout my life without even knowing they were real. Isn't that an epiphany.

After getting married, another more enlightening experience was with my family while searching for a home, driving around in the country. We happened to find this place by chance, driving by as we were visiting friends in Lockport, another small community that I adored. We found this beautiful country home in a nice community. I felt so blessed to have found this gorgeous home with its winding driveway and beautiful, lush perennial gardens and fruit trees. It was a paradise and took my breath away, especially since it was close to the city but still far enough away from the hustle and bustle of the city.

Besides this beautiful oasis in our backyard, we were a five-minute drive from a luscious green provincial park that had the best man-made pool and bicycle trails on earth. We frequented it at least once a week. It also had the most beautiful, serene campground that we still go to every summer in our awesome recreation vehicle. Its breathtaking beauty and natural landscapes provide my escape to nature.

Our driveway was a beautiful path of fruit trees, and we eventually put up a fenced-in corral so that we could board horses and have sheep of our own. We also put up a chicken coop and raised chickens. It was so wonderful to have these and be so in tune with nature. We also had cougars, wolves, fox, and wild dogs to be extra cautious of. Unfortunately, some dogs killed one of our cats, whom I really loved. I miss her so much; her name was Ami, and she was so beautiful and affectionate. I'm sure she was one of my guardian angels with her perfect white fur and crystal blue eyes.

Not only did this home feel like a Garden of Eden, as it was gorgeously landscaped, but the neighbors were also a godsend, and some were a bit eccentric.

We soon found out that some of our neighbors were wonderful Christian people, and they became our good friends. I loved them dearly. I was so grateful that they offered to become our children's caregivers, as we both had to commute to the city for work. At this time in my life, I was a bit frazzled but felt so blessed, and I thanked the universe for placing us there. The neighbors we had were so welcoming and helpful to us the whole time we lived there. I felt truly blessed.

A variety of individuals lived in our neighborhood. On one side of us were two ladies who had horses and loved animals as much as

I did. I became friends with them and loved visiting and riding the horses and taking care of the animals.

On the other side of us was a family who attempted to run an exotic animal shelter/business and housed in their shed a tiger, monkeys, snakes, lizards, spiders, and more. I believe they even had an alligator or crocodile living in their bathroom and iguanas in their living room. They also had two young children, and I thought it was not very safe for them. I believe someone in the neighborhood did not appreciate them being there and called the authorities on them, who eventually shut them down.

The neighbor on the other side of this house was a very nice, middle-aged gentleman who enjoyed our company and welcomed us over. He had a pool and allowed us to use it whenever we wanted, even when he wasn't home. The kids and their friends and I had so much enjoyment, and I am so grateful to have known him. It was an oasis for us with his parklike setting.

We also enjoyed spending time at this gentleman's yard because he also loved animals of all breeds. He had shelters built for outdoor cats all over his yard and beautiful peacocks that he kept in a coop in his backyard. It was another paradise to be admired.

The neighbors on the other side of him had large dogs. I believe they were Doberman and shepherds. Even though I was not afraid of them, my kids and other people were. They lived at the end of our driveway, which we frequently walked down. We had to pass by their yard, and the dogs would bark and lunge at us. Once I got to know the owners, I asked if they could keep them more secure inside their property. They were very nice and decided to put up an electric fence, which worked beautifully.

It turned out that two families who lived across the road from us were Christians, and they were such friendly and down-to-earth people. They soon convinced us that it was what we needed in our life. My partner at the time, who was also programmed to believe in the church doctrine, became friends with the pastor. He encouraged us to join their church. He convinced us that we had to work on our salvation and become born again. It was an evangelical Baptist church that followed the doctrine of Christianity.

Ironically, the couple who lived next door to them were into wiccan and other alternative spiritual practices. She made soaps and lotions and potions that I was so intrigued with. I wanted so much to be friends with her but was discouraged from it by other people in the neighborhood and my husband. We did invite them over for a gathering once, and that was when we found out what their religion was. I wished I could have gotten to know them better.

As you can imagine, I was enthralled by the variety of people in our neighborhood and became friends with most of them. It wasn't easy being social while having to work full-time and taking care of my family. But in those days, I seemed to have more energy to be outdoors, and I believe my kids made it so much easier for me to get out there more, not only to socialize but to scrutinize who our neighbors were. I was very protective of my kids and very particular about the people they associated with.

While attending church, I loved the people we met and the community it offered. But I still wasn't feeling enlightened or aware of my spiritual higher self yet. I even became baptized in the hope that the spirit of the divine would save me from myself. I guess I just wasn't ready to face my demons at the time and wallowed in my brokenness. It didn't help that my marriage was on the rocks due to our power struggles and offensive behaviors to each other. I eventually left this home and ended up in a woman's shelter, where I found the peace and clarity I needed to move forward.

Through my current spiritual development, I am learning that we are all born from this higher power known as God, from the spiritual plane that gives us our divine essence or soul. We start out in life as innocent beings, and then life comes at us, sometimes gracefully and other times with a vengeance. Mine started out in a fairy land of wonderment and magic, where I was free to be me. Although my upbringing wasn't the most nurturing, I did have a mother who trusted my abilities to wander about freely. She allowed me the freedom to explore and learn from my environment, which eventually bit me in the behind a few times.

I believe I must have had angels with me, considering some of the places and predicaments I was in; I am thankful to be alive.

CHAPTER 8

Coming to Terms with More Family Drama

"I see my parents as tiny children who need love –
I have compassion for my parents' childhoods. I now know
that I chose them because they were perfect for what I had to
learn. I forgive them and set them free, and I set myself free."

Power Thought Cards – Louise Hay

As I previously mentioned, I was born into a family that had dysfunctional tendencies. Later I learned that most families experience at least some of these shadows known as emotional, physical, and sexual abuse, addiction, jealousy, violence, poverty, illness, abandonment, and betrayal.

To this day, I still realize how much of an impact those karmic experiences had on me. After losing my innocence as a child and then well into my adolescence and adulthood, the karmic ties have affected my perception of reality. Living with shame and denial of the past, I felt like a broken person. Although there were many negative experiences that my family karma had to endure, I've come to realize that they can affect you in either a positive or negative way, depending on your attitude. You'll either become:

- on the positive side, victorious and empowered or,
- on the negative side, passive, aggressive, and bitter.

I swayed between these two sides as I became and grew into my own person. Being raised in a home where poverty and scarcity were the norm, with very little spiritual connection, I wasn't exactly on the right track of enlightenment. I was also not taught in a positive or self-honoring way to deal with my emotions and setbacks in life. Because I was not allowed to express my feelings and emotions, I became passive-aggressive and bitter when faced with any stressful events or obstacles. I became paralyzed with fear whenever someone confronted me with an issue of any kind.

Once I came to realize that the abuse I had endured was not my fault, I was set free and relieved. A lifetime of shame was lifted, and I was free to be me. On my spiritual development journey, I eventually became empowered with the awareness of my higher self. I began to heal, understand, and grow. My knowledge of the divine creator of all, God, and communication with my spirit guides have led me through these abuses to a more peaceful and wonderous, rich life.

As was so eloquently explained and taught to me by a wise spiritual teacher named Sara Wiseman:

If you don't release yourself from family karma, you can't become free. At some point, every conscious person has to come to grips with their family of origin—at whatever level of drama and dysfunction— and figure out how they can heal ...

The first aspect of releasing family karma is about the belief system. When we're born, we arrive into religions, cultures, and belief systems that our family teaches us. But the journey to be an adult is to decide what you think—not what you're told to believe. That's one part—releasing the family karma means releasing old beliefs and determining what you yourself believe.

The second part of family karma work is about releasing all the hurts and wounds. Many people have experienced abuse in their families. This process is about learning to not be a victim. We need to understand what happened, claim it as our experience, and then decide we won't ever experience this again. If we were abused in our family, releasing ourselves from family karma means stepping into our own power, now and forever.

As mentioned earlier, my experiences in my life's journey with family and friends were filled with all kinds of drama and disillusion— from the exploration of uncharted territories to the exhilaration of my own desires, which sometimes brought disappointment and grief and sometimes love and happiness. As a sensitive, empathic being, I felt in my heart that I was placed in this world of contrasting desires and expectations to experience more love, joy, and peace in my life.

In fact, looking back, I began to understand the lessons life had to teach me with all the drama in my family life and with friends from an early age. Even though I was taught to believe that I was to settle for what life lessons dealt me, I refused to settle for second best.

If only I had known how to spread the message of our divine essence and spiritual being. If only I had known earlier in life what we are here for, that is to spread love and light into the world. I could have tried harder to be a person of light and love for my three older brothers and sister who have all passed on from their own struggles to find meaning in this world.

If only we could be reminded that, as spiritual beings, we need companionship and soul mates to support us on our journey to self-discovery. We need to realize that our self-worth and participation in life is meaningful and needed, before we hit rock bottom—before we become so entrenched in our miseries and addictions that we no longer have hope for our future.

This is how I understood my siblings at times, especially my younger sister, whom I loved dearly but let down so many times. She was a chronic alcoholic who didn't see her worthiness shine through, though I did. When she was sober, she was such a beautiful, loving soul and had so much wisdom. I wanted so much for us to be friends and experience things together, but it was not going to happen. Unfortunately, it was too late to make amends for this to happen, as we were not always friendly to each other. I guess it all started when we were kids. She was my mother's favorite, or so it appeared to me at the time.

When I look back, and to this day, everyone in my mom's family, including my older brothers, took precedence over me, or so my ego convinced me to believe. I couldn't bond with her, so maybe I was resentful of that most of the time. I felt unloved, neglected, and berated most times. I know I was loving though because I felt love for all my siblings, though I was too afraid to be vocal or show my emotions.

I sometimes felt that she was resentful toward me. Being spiteful is an annoying shadow of our family. It is something I had to deal with and confront on many occasions, as I know I felt jealousy of others myself. I know for sure that most women I tried to form relationships with shunned me. Maybe it was due to my tenacious, happy-go-lucky nature. I really did believe that I was more of an asset than a hindrance to my family and friends' lives and wanted only to be loved by them.

My sister was a couple of years younger than I, and she couldn't keep up with me physically. So, I resented it when my mother asked that I take her along with me while playing outdoors. I would do my best to ditch her and would only play indoors with her, but I did really want to be her companion. As we became adults, these feelings still lingered, and I pushed her away. I only hope that she can forgive me as I have forgiven her and myself for our altercations.

We did have some fond times and memories together, despite our desolate upbringing. My favorite ones were teaching my sister how to dress, read, cook, and so on. I even loved playing school and being her teacher and singing songs to her, especially at bedtime. I was a tomboy at heart and didn't especially enjoy playing with dolls and such.

As I grew and had my own family, I had more of an appreciation for my family. I tried to invite her and her family back into it. However, due to our substance abuse and addictions, most times we ended up in conflict and disagreement on matters. As much as I loved my family and wanted to see them happy, I had to learn to have boundaries in my life. I had to realize that their self-destructive behaviors were theirs, and only they could choose to be healthy and whole.

No matter how much I tried to be a caretaker and role model for my family, I realized that I am a WIP (work in progress) and need self-care. I see the patterns of dysfunction and neediness in my past and current relationships, which are sometimes the result of our upbringing. Sometimes we just need to be accepted where we are on our healing journey.

In a course I took called Communication Secrets for a Happy Relationship, Ariel Ford explained:

> Our unconscious need is to have our feelings of aliveness and wholeness restored by someone who reminds us of our caretakers. In other words, we look for someone with the same deficits of care and

attention that hurt us in the first place. So, when we fall in love, when bells ring and the world seems altogether a better place, our old brain is telling us that we've found someone with whom we can finally get our needs met. Unfortunately, since we don't understand what's going on, we're shocked when the awful truth of our beloved surfaces, and our first impulse is to run screaming in the opposite direction.

Having a soulmate is a beautiful dance towards wholeness if you're willing to allow and learn from the inevitable messy bumps that go with the territory of being in a relationship. The great news is you are no longer a child. You are an adult who is fully equipped to move beyond those original wounds to a deeper center within yourself. Your soulmate is like a companion on your way to that place of healing.

According to another author named Hendrix:

It is the image of the person who can make me whole again. We find partners who help us complete the unfinished business of childhood. Our adult relationships and struggles feel familiar because they remind us of our primary caretakers. These relationships present us with the opportunity to heal past wounds and find deep relational fulfillment. But it's an opportunity, not a guarantee.

I know now that my relationships with my family and partners were to provide me with the life lessons to enable me to see beyond our imperfections, as we are all created in the same image as God intended.

CHAPTER 9

Coming out of the Cave and Seeing the Light

"I am taking the next step for my healing
– The moment I say positive affirmations, I step out of the victim
role. I am no longer helpless. I acknowledge my own power."

Wisdom Cards – Louise Hay

With a programmed mind-set of lack and believing that life was supposed to be a struggle, I struggled to survive from month to month or paycheck to paycheck. Even though I felt stuck in this way of thinking, I still knew in my heart and soul that life could and should be better. I knew that God would not allow us to suffer to the point of passing unless that was something we wanted to happen (as was the case with my siblings). However, with all that I'd already been through, my battle scars were already showing up as chronic fatigue and depression, and I was only in my early twenties.

What are the symptoms of fibro? As defined by the WRHA in Canada.

> Pain is the main symptom. The aches, pains and stiffness in muscles, joints and soft tissues vary from day to day or week to week. The pain also tends to move from one part of the body to another. It is most common in the neck, shoulders, chest, arms, legs, hips and back. Other common symptoms are tiredness, headache and problems with the digestive system, especially trouble swallowing, recurrent abdominal pain or diarrhea.

Without giving in to the victim mentality, I went on with my life, with all its struggles and the symptoms mentioned above, and I realized that I needed to change my perspective on life. After all, I had my dream job(s) and my beautiful home(s) and family(s), with all the traditions, and rebellion against the traditions.

I did not like to complain about my aches and pains, for my life on the outside appeared lovely, and I considered my current reality a blessing. I was good at faking it until you make it, and my wonderful life was magnificent, with all the material comforts it could offer.

I believe that I have manifested my imperfect soul mates into my life and that life was only meant to get better, better, and better—but not without further struggles and lessons to learn, of course.

I suffered in silence, as people with fibromyalgia experience aches and tenderness throughout the body that is not noticeable on the outside. This tenderness is mainly caused by inflammation and is most noticed at certain places called tender points. Tender points are specific places on the neck, shoulders, back, hips, arms, and legs. These points hurt when pressure is put on them. This is how I was officially diagnosed by a neurosurgeon who tested my nerves and muscle reactions to applied pressure.

Even though my body was in constant pain and fatigue, my life appeared picture-perfect on the outside. My life was wonderful, but I was still feeling all the symptoms and depression from not being well. My life became a roller coaster of ups and downs. After taking certain medications for pain and antidepressants to help me sleep, I was left in a fog of discontent, not knowing who I was to become. I began to study natural remedies. I did not have faith in the pharmaceutical world.

I somehow knew that things would get better if only I could get my strength and energy back. I thought maybe if I didn't have to work, I could rest more and be without stress. I thought of going on disability for depression or fibromyalgia, but I did not want these illnesses to define me. I couldn't live comfortably with that. I took a mental health day on occasion and found them to be so beneficial in helping me to cope. I was blessed to have a job that gave me the benefits to do this. I don't know how I would have survived otherwise.

I also felt much better after a prolonged vacation, as I had some time to myself. I felt a little selfish at times, but I would insist that my kids go to camp during summer vacations just so that I could be by myself. There were times when they didn't want to, but I believe once they were at camp, they always had a wonderful time.

I know for sure that I loved going away as a child, if only to get away from the chaos at home. In fact, as I reminisce, it was so much fun going to camp or other people's homes for a week or two. I remember going with my aunt one time. She was a couple of years older than I and so lively and outgoing. I thought, *Wow, we're going to have such a great time together.* Well, on our way to the camp we were going to, she started bawling and wanting to stay behind. I was so surprised, as I didn't think she was losing anyone or anything by going on this trip. She had just as much if not more chaos at her home as I did. I tried to comfort her and advised her that we were going to have a great time together. She finally calmed down, and we spent the next two weeks together having a wonderful time at camp.

Even at those times, I felt protected, and with the help of my divine spirit guides, life was full of wonder and exploration, never ceasing to amaze me.

After reading through this memoir again, it's beginning to sound pretty Woo, Woo or out there, but it's my story and I'm sticking with it. LOL.

CHAPTER 10

Dealing with the Skeletons in the Closet and Driving through Life in the Wrong Lane

"I take a deep breath and allow myself to relax. My whole body calms down. – It does not matter what other people say or do. What matters is how I choose to react and what I choose to believe about myself."

I can do it cards – Louise Hay

One of the coping remedies I found to help alleviate or take away my aches and pains and weariness was consumption of alcohol and using other prescribed and OTC drugs as medicine. I drank almost daily to self-medicate when I was feeling pain and headaches, and although it helped in the moment, I didn't like how I felt the next day or the fogginess and disconnection from spirit I felt, not to mention the weight that I put on.

Smoking or ingesting cannabis was a bit more soothing but again left me groggy and debilitated the next day. After a while, I was never sure whether I was feeling lousy due to the dis-ease or the side effects of self-medicating. Every time I tried to do without, I experienced excruciating headaches. I knew intuitively at a cellular level that I could not go on day after day using these substances and still live to be healthy and vibrant.

> People with fibromyalgia are more likely to have anxiety, chronic headaches and symptoms worsened by weather, mental stress or poor sleep. Other symptoms that you may experience include trouble sleeping through the night, problems thinking or remembering things, feeling depressed or anxious and feeling dizzy or light-headed. As defined by the WRHA in Canada.

Unfortunately, the symptoms may get worse when you overexert yourself or when the weather is damp and cold. However, I was urged by my physician to not let this prevent me from doing some type of physical activity. I find the best natural remedy for this condition is activity. Even a few minutes of walking, dancing, or yoga will do wonders for your body as well as your spirit.

> Since there is no single diagnostic test for fibromyalgia, your health care provider should review your medical history and your patterns of symptoms and may need a second opinion of a neuro specialist to confirm the diagnosis. As defined by the WRHA in Canada.

Don't ever be afraid to ask your health care provider to examine you while observing places that are tender. Whatever you are going through, don't ever give up on yourself and your thoughts and feelings as they are yours to be acknowledged.

Even though these symptoms persist in my life, I feel now that I can at least remedy some of them by taking supplements like omega-3 and curcumin (turmeric) for inflammation of the joints, having short naps when necessary, meditating, practicing Reiki and other energy-healing modalities, reading inspirational messages, and developing my intuitive abilities.

Even though you may not feel well enough, it is best to stay positive and work on your spirituality and connection to loved ones and your community or tribe (whoever you choose those to be). Your immediate family may not be the best support that your soul needs at this time. So, like me, you may have to be brave and go outside of your comfort zone to connect with others.

That may mean joining a spiritual organization, getting together with peers at work, or volunteering. The benefits of spreading your light and love are immense. I know from experience that this is the hardest to do when you are not feeling the energy to do it, but it is essential.

Even going to church can be uplifting in the darkest of moments. Hopefully it is a church that supports you even though you are imperfect, rather than condemning you for being a sinner. This is how I felt most times after going to the congregation that we belonged to. Maybe it was my tainted attitude about organized religion due to past experiences. I knew I wasn't perfect and never would be, so I just fell into a deeper depression whenever that was made apparent.

Most times, I considered myself a moral individual with some skeletons in the closet and baggage from prior negative experiences that most of us have. I knew I needed and wanted counselling from someone but not through the church. Although I was ready to discuss my problems and surrender to God, I wasn't ready to face my demons.

When I realized that the only option for controlling my illness was using prescription drugs with their many side effects, I felt defeated but also strangely empowered. I thought that by following the doctor's orders and taking my meds, I would at least get through some of the daily struggles I was having at the time, and I would only take them for as long as I needed to.

I started to consider my long-term health and wanted to live a more vibrant life. I started exercising more and felt it was the only true relief I got. One of my exercise routines is to dance at least two to five times per week and always like nobody's watching. I have been so fortunate in life to have partners who love to dance. I guess it was one of my strong character traits that I would not live without. I am convinced that is how I met and was attracted to each partner that has been a part of my dance of life.

I've always loved to dance, and I remember, as a little girl, dancing with my family and friends in our living room—doing the cha-cha, rumba, waltz, or free style. I especially loved going to our community dances and found so much joy and excitement there.

As I got older, I started dancing in nightclubs, and it made me feel free and alive. However much I loved dancing and socializing, I did not like the nightlife crowd at the clubs once people started overdrinking or doing drugs. It was okay up to a certain point, and then I had to leave. I am thankful that I had enough sense to know that overindulgence in alcohol is not a pretty sight for anyone. Even though at times I had tendencies to overindulge, I don't know for sure if I was reckless. I knew it was not the life that I wanted. I found other ways to enjoy without all the hype and intoxication that the nightlife brought on and out of people.

The people I got to know while taking dance lessons and becoming involved in the various groups and community of dancers were so friendly. As most of these dancers don't drink alcohol, hanging out with them was so much healthier than going to the nightclubs. I felt so blessed to have them in my life. Once involved, I vowed to not give it up, and dancing was one of the traits I considered when idealizing (or manifesting) my new partner.

In addition to that, he had to be kind, patient, generous, outgoing, adventurous (in a healthy way), spontaneous, and, most importantly, spiritual. With the help of my divine spirit guides and other spiritual teachers and authors, I believe I found those people for a reason. I am still a WIP and learning to be a more loving, spiritual being and learning to manifest what my heart desires in a healthy way.

CHAPTER 11

More Bumps and Potholes in the Road

"I release all criticism.
I only give out that which I wish to receive in return. My love
and acceptance of others is mirrored to me in every moment."

Power Thought Cards – Louise Hay

Around 2005, my partner at the time surprised me with a night out for my forty-something birthday. He decided we would take Latin dance lessons. Well, I was so excited and intrigued by this gesture and was especially excited that we had both found a new passion in life. It was something we could do together, as we didn't have many things in common.

Although I loved the excitement and energy of Latin dancing, especially the salsa, it was not an easy dance to learn, and there were times I came away from it in tears of frustration.

Even though I felt I was doing a terrific job, we didn't seem to be dancing well together. If it weren't for our agreement to dance with others with no qualms, I would have given up in frustration. I recall one time we were out at a club, and we weren't enjoying each other's company. I was in tears, ready to call it quits, when a friend of ours who was also new to the dance community asked me to dance. He was such a great lead and so encouraging that I fell in love with the dance all over again. Not that my husband wasn't a good lead; I was just too insulted by him to trust him enough to lead me at the time.

It was the most memorable time of our lives together. We both shared a passion in life that wasn't so passive but lively, and maybe at times a little too dramatic. We finally had a passion to pursue something that we both enjoyed. We took lessons constantly and were taught how to do salsa, cha-cha, meringue, nightclub, country two-step, and more. It was so much fun and exciting to be around various types of people, young and young at heart. I met some wonderful people who encouraged me to stick with it. I believed it could save our marriage, but I guess there was just too much water under the bridge. This dance of life that we knew was not always easy, but I wouldn't change it either way.

While we were dancing and trying to make our marriage work, I was still dealing with depression and chronic fatigue syndrome and taking antidepressants. I was not living in our family home because I decided that I needed another break (this being around the sixth time) from our chaotic family life to try to find the meaning of my own.

Even though my daughters were my life and motivation at the time, I decided it was best to leave them with their dad so that they could continue their life with the least amount of disruption. I lived close by in a cute little apartment down the road. I continued to take them to their extracurricular activities and school events.

Being in this rocky marriage was not uplifting for either of us. By this time, we had been together for eighteen years. Our girls were fifteen and sixteen at the time, and since we never went out much while they were younger, we decided it was time to go out on dates and do something for ourselves, to do something fun and healthy.

We kept up with the dancing for about two years, while trying to get over past hurts. We continued with ongoing sarcastic interactions. To say the least, we did not empower our growth or understanding for each other or the life we had together. We realized that both of us had deep emotional pain and family karma to deal with and so began our spiritual journeys together and apart. We were both so weary at the time and not very pleasant to each other. We tried our hardest to overlook our imperfections and resentments to make it work, but unfortunately it wasn't enough.

While we were both working on our spiritualty within the church, I attended counselling and did my own soul searching. I'm sure I've read every self-help book out there, including the scriptures, *The Secret*, Dr. Phil, *Oprah* magazine, Hay House books and affirmation cards, and more. But they did not yet answer my questions of why am I here and what is my true purpose in life?

I felt so enlivened and empowered to live a more positive life but at the same time overwhelmed with the roles in my life: being the care provider to my children and the caretaker for my mother and siblings, while holding a full-time job. It was all I could handle at the time. I was running on empty but still willing to step into the unknown, out of my comfort zone. I believed I could cope with whatever changes I needed to make to discover who I truly was and could be.

I knew I needed help and support but wasn't sure where or who could provide it. I still had hope for the future, even though I knew I had to make changes in my life to become freer. I needed guidance or spiritual intervention. I believe that staying positive and optimistic about the future was what I needed to constantly work on to get by. It's far better to have an optimistic attitude toward the challenges we face than be weighed down by disappointment, worry, and self-pity.

I found many uplifting, encouraging words in *The Secret,* Jack Canfield's *Key to Living the Law of Attraction,* numerous Hay House books, e-books, audio books, cards, and courses that gave me faith in the divine.

One of the first inspirational books I purchased and I just love was by Jack Canfield and D.D. Watkins, a law of attraction gift set that included the following:

- *Key to Living the Law of Attraction: A Simple Guide to Creating the Life of Your Dreams*
- *Gratitude Daily Journal* that helps me to honor and appreciate the abundance in my life
- a vision board

With these tools, I was able to manifest new people and family into my life who enjoyed things that I enjoyed, like dancing, singing, traveling, camping (or glamping) in our RV, and getting together for potlucks. I've traveled and seen so many different places in the last few years with the wonderful soul mate I am now with. Life is great and always an adventure.

CHAPTER 12

On Finding My Higher Self

"I am connected with a HIGHER POWER.
- The wisdom and intelligence of the
UNIVERSE IS MINE TO USE.
I trust in Life to support me.

Heart Thoughts Cards – Louise Hay

I have always been a strong believer in my spirit guides, angels, and the supernatural or magic of the universe. However, because of the strong doctrine of the church we attended, I didn't feel empowered by the Holy Spirit that everyone else was seeming to master. I felt spiritually depleted and at the time did not have it in me to develop my intuitive and healing abilities. I instead stayed in the spiritual closet and kept believing that my life would have more peace and joy to come.

After reading *The Secret* and Jack Canfield's *Law of Attraction*, a guide to creating the life of your dreams, I started journaling and manifesting the kind of life I envisioned for myself and my family. I even included my significant other, and although he did start to become more tolerant and respectful of me, I still could not get on the same page as him. I began to realize that we did not have the same values and dreams in life.

Due to my incapacity to bond with this individual, and since we were both self-absorbed and my mental health issues began to fester in my physical body, I felt it necessary to separate and do some soul searching. Unfortunately, people who are egotistical control freaks do not change easily, no matter how much spiritual counselling they receive. These wounded soul mates could not appreciate the connection they had. They were meant to help encourage each other but instead grew apart. Because of wounds that were already too deep to heal and because of our trust issues, our connection to each other was shattered beyond repair. Our resentments from what had transpired in our past lives took their toll, and it was not possible at the time to reconcile.

After great soul searching, I decided this relationship was not a good fit for either of us. I was getting more sick and tired by the day, to the point that I thought I was going to have an early demise. I was way too young to feel that sick, old, and defeated.

I was determined not to let this sickness get the best of me, as I wanted to make my life a success, and I wanted to have a joyous life. I started realizing that there is so much to live for in our short life span on earth. It was around this time that I read the book *The Secret* and started working on my spirituality, realizing that I had unmet needs and dreams to fulfill.

I started to realize and believe that if a person does not have any passions in life or dreams to aspire to, they may be prone to an early departure or just become so cynical that no one wants to be around them. Although I was still disillusioned with what my life was and should be, I knew in my heart that it could be better, if only I could get my passion for life back.

When I decided to leave my relationship and create a life for myself, my girls were seventeen and eighteen years old. I think prior to this we had both already left the marriage emotionally and physically, as we were not sharing the same bedroom. I also had left the home at least seven times for various reasons, primarily to find myself again. As we've been advised by most relationship experts out there, relationships are a lot of work and require you to be honest to yourself and your partner. When there is any doubt, fear, or resentment present, honesty will become next to impossible, and your efforts will become hindered.

Prior to this, each time I left, we would reconcile, and I believed that things would change and be better for us. Most times, they were better, and we were happy together as a family. Life always did get better for us, but there was always that lingering resentment. I was in the victim mode in this dance of the illusion of the white picket fence and traditional family. I wanted so much to have a happy, healthy, traditional family that I endured living under the veil of illusion and gave up my power to grow emotionally and spiritually.

But, with my belief in divinity tools such as horoscopes, numerology, and tarot/oracle cards, as well as the synchronistic ways of the divine, I was given hope. I began to rely on these more to enlighten my life and to keep me on the right path to joy, peace, and happiness. I've been relying on them for more than forty-five years now, and they never cease to amaze me with how accurate they can be in determining which path to follow or change.

I believe that we are all on a spiritual path to enlightenment and will express our soul gifts as they become more apparent to us on our soul's journey.

CHAPTER 13

Growing Up with Family Dramas

"Freedom is my Divine Right
- I am free to think wonderful thoughts. I move
beyond the past limitations into freedom.
I am now becoming all that I am created to be."

Power Thought Cards – Louise hay

While growing up in a not so friendly environment, I experienced verbal and physical violence and became afraid of any kind of verbal threat or violence. Experiencing traumatic events such as my uncles fighting in my grandma's home, with blood flowing everywhere, I was a bit traumatized.

Also, seeing my aunt (who is now deceased) in a hospital bed, unrecognizable after being beat up by her partner, among other physical and verbal abuse that I experienced, was all so very distressing.

Due to past traumatic physical and verbal abuse experienced in my life, I became very untrusting of my former partner's intentions whenever we argued. I was terrified of any possibility of physical violence and couldn't tolerate loud confrontations, which again was part of my victimhood mentality. Add to that a very loud, demanding voice, whether anger was present or not. I was afraid and withdrew from confrontations with him. I was unable to see through their own troubling fears and needs and was unable to accept it, as we were sensitive individuals wanting validation for our existence.

I know my meekness and inability to express my needs has caused a lot of frustration in my former relationships. I want to acknowledge that I forgive them and myself for not being able to accept and understand our own mental, emotional, and spiritual needs. I do realize now that we all come from families with karmic ties that need healing.

Due to my own karma that had to be dealt with, I must admit I wasn't the easiest person to live with, and I take fifty percent responsibility for our marital problems. I was also self-centered, controlling, and demanding and did not know how to voice my needs in an assertive, constructive manner. Because of my chronic fatigue syndrome and depression, I became very moody and isolated myself from any type of relationships and the outside world. I found ways to cope that were not healthy, and I knew if I didn't change or heal, I was not going to live the long, healthy, and vibrant life that I deserved and wanted.

I am now realizing that there are a lot of ways in life to find enjoyment and pleasure. My current partner and I have found many activities that we can do together besides our dancing. We love to golf, bowl, doing indoor and outdoor walking, traveling, and glamping in our RV.

I also love to practice my card readings, energy healings, meditation, and yoga, and I appreciate the energy healing and synchronicities they provide. I'm still a work in process, but I am having a more adventurous and joyous life experience, and I have faith that more is yet to come. I am also not afraid of death, as I once was, and I believe that there is more on the other side to look forward to.

In fact, I am fascinated by the accuracy of the divination cards that I continue to practice with. I someday hope to come out of the spiritual closet and do readings for others, like I have in the past, to assist them on their sacred journey. I have already chosen my name and registered it under yourdivineinspirations.com. I am so excited for the future. It is such an exciting journey that I've always dreamed of.

I received my first card deck when I was around twenty-eight or so, from my former partner. At that time, I did some readings for others and on myself. However, again, with my day job and evenings spent looking after my family, I had no energy left to pursue this further so put them aside.

I continue to seek spiritual divine counselling through workshops and spiritual-development groups. I also continue to use the tarot and oracle card readings to improve my intuitive ability to provide divine inspiration to others. I hope I will impact their lives the way that I've been impacted and guided throughout my life. Today I am almost embarrassed to admit that I have roughly forty decks or so and have practiced over the last thirty years. I will continue to read and take workshops on how to become better at providing this psychic/intuitive means of soul searching, especially by connecting to our higher power and the source of our energy and abundance from the divine creator, God.

My new passions in life are to coach others in health and wellness while using other healing modalities that can assist them on their sacred journey.

If you'd like to learn more, please visit my website at Yourdivineinspirations.com.

CHAPTER 14

My Life between Worlds

"Don't Make Assumptions
– Find the courage to ask questions and to express what
you really want. Communicate with others as clearly as you
can to avoid misunderstandings, sadness, and dramas.
With just this one agreement, you can
completely transform your life."

The Four Agreements – Don Migual Ruiz

I was so proud to be a mother and wife throughout my life and was so grateful for the life I had. I lived in the most beautiful home in a prestigious neighborhood, which I believe I manifested from the dreams I previously envisioned. It was a three-thousand-square-foot home with three finished floors. We each had our own bathroom, and my bedroom was a 350-square-foot posh suite. The walls were primarily white until I painted them neutral. It had a beautiful European-style kitchen with all stainless steel appliances, beautiful ceramic floors, and tons of windows with etched glass throughout. It reminded me of the ivory tower, and I was the princess of the North End; at least that's what I was told by many.

Leaving this lifestyle and our family was the hardest and most heartbreaking decision I've had to make in my sacred journey. I loved my life, my home, and my family and felt so guilty for having to break it up, but I felt if I didn't, I was going to die from exhaustion. I was so sick and tired at the time and knew that being in this relationship was not healthy for me or my family.

At this time, although I considered myself a strong-willed woman, I also suffered from low self-esteem and gave away my power to others.

I believed, or my ego believed, that people would think less of me for leaving a life that appeared perfect. I must admit that he was a good person most times—a person with integrity, who also had a sense of humor and steadfastness about him. He made things happen, with my monetary help too of course, as we went from living in a subsidized housing project to owning beautiful acreages in the country and then moving to the most prestigious neighborhood I had ever imagined. I still remember saving diligently for our down payment.

I recognized early on in our relationship that we both wanted to be the breadwinner of the family and both liked to have control of things. I thought it was a good character trait, and I admired it, but I eventually learned to resent it since I also considered myself the breadwinner. And so the power struggle began. Although he was good at making a living, he failed to recognize that I too contributed and had some input into what we were set to accomplish together.

I felt completely unacknowledged and devalued for what we had built together, even though I worked hard out of the home and had complete responsibility for our home. I worked full-time and contributed to the household chores and took care of the bills. He took care of the vehicles and any major home renovations. I did all the grocery shopping, cooking, and housework with the help of my kids. I also was the main chauffer and took them to school and extracurricular activities. I didn't mind driving them, as I found that driving my kids around was the best and only time we could talk and when they would open up to me about their lives.

I also seemed to be the only one who was interested in connecting with our families. I loved having or going to family get-togethers, even though I was nervous about socializing. Celebrating birthdays, Christmas, or just having dinner together was so special, and I was so grateful to all my in-laws who provided these opportunities. I did not mind doing these things, as they were all part of my wonderful family life experiences. All the times I had with my family were all worth it to me, and I loved it and still miss them.

I still loved him but had to stop feeling responsible for his happiness in life, because I knew that was his to find. I wanted more out of life and just wanted my life back. I wanted to travel to exotic places with my friends and family, do more activities, and of course work on my spirituality. Even if that meant giving up our beautiful home for me to afford these things, I needed to change my perspective on how I viewed life. I knew we weren't on the same page, because whenever I mentioned my dreams, he would try to convince me otherwise and would despise me for even trying to change the way things were.

Even though it appeared that I had the perfect life of luxury, it was not so leisurely, and I was struggling on the inside. I wanted to be genuine and have authentic friendships, but I was so caught up in my own difficult times and unhappiness that I didn't want to burden anyone with my problems. So, I isolated myself until I could not continue this way any longer.

CHAPTER 15

Exploring My Soul's Calling and Purpose in Life

"I Release the Past and Forgive Everyone
– I free myself and everyone in my life from old past hurts.
They are free and I am free to move into
new, glorious experiences."

Power Thought Cards – Louise Hay

I was always in search of someone to confide in besides my faithful comrades at work. I'm sure they thought I was a messed-up housewife from the hills. Fortunately, I had access to an employee assistance plan. I could access family counselling, that I attended on numerous occasions, if only to vent my frustrations. As I did not have a very healthy support system or anyone I could talk to outside of work.

I also spent time in a few women's shelters and grew spiritually from these experiences. The counsellors there were wonderful, and I felt so at peace while staying there. They recommended group counselling, and I attended a few sessions with various other women who were going through the same belligerent situations as I was. I thank God for these programs and institutions and, of course, the divine intervention for presenting these opportunities.

Although I didn't want any more drama in my life, I knew I had to hash out the past to move forward in a positive light. I had to learn how to forgive those who had mistreated me, and I had to forgive myself for allowing those wrongdoings. I became empowered and set free. I had a better understanding of why this was happening to me and my part in it. I was able to grow spiritually with gratitude and compassion for myself and others.

Even though I am not perfect, I still know that my soul is ready and calling to expand. As Rebecca Campbell, another Hay House author, advises:

> I am ready to take a leap of faith and expand my soul's calling. All the gifts, strength, power and light are within me. Once I get out of my own way, I can become what I was meant to be.
>
> Amen.

CHAPTER 16

No More Drama Please

"All My Relationships are Enveloped in a Circle of Love
- I HAVE WONDERFUL, HARMONIOUS RELATIONSHIPS
With everyone, where there is mutual
respect and caring on both sides

Heart Thought Cards – Louise Hay

Soon after leaving my marriage and living on my own, my girls decided to move out west. I was left with another broken heart and feeling of abandonment to deal with. My girls were my world, and when they left, I felt so much remorse and regret. I felt I was a complete failure as a wife and a parent. I immediately went into grief counselling, which helped me to overcome this breakup and the feelings of abandonment and guilt. Through it all, I have become a stronger person.

I moved into a cozy little home and bought my own vehicle, as my ex seized the beater of a car that I was driving while we were together. A friend that I met helped me find the most beautiful car that I've ever owned. And I made new friends along the way.

It was very synchronistic how I found my new home. I first moved into an apartment. It had an indoor pool, gym, indoor parking, and security, which made me feel safe. It was a beautiful apartment, besides the long walk from the elevator. Most times I just walked the four flights of stairs from the underground parking, so I did get my exercise in. It also had a very small kitchenette, with very few cupboards and one of those apartment-sized fridges that I could never understand. Don't these developers realize that people in apartments need room in their cupboards and fridge as much as anyone else? Besides the little annoyances, I loved it. I thought it was nice and welcoming, and it would do for the time being.

I was so used to living in a larger-than-life house with my own master suite, garage, yard, and so on. But I needed to find a place I could call a home of my own. So, even though it was January and very cold in our neck of the woods, I ventured out to find a home. I didn't hear much from the realtor that I had engaged to find me something. I decided one day that I would go and find something on my own.

Since I was already practicing the power of attraction and manifesting, I thought that the perfect home for me was out there. I even had my list of all the necessities that I required to make me feel content. One day I decided to drive around the area I wanted to live in. Well, I found a place that had a few of my requirements. It was a little side-by-side with a fully fenced yard and a double garage. Although the main level was the size of my former bedroom suite, I needed to accept this new phase, this next chapter of my life, with a positive outlook.

I thought it was perfect and what I could afford at the time, so I put in an offer. The next day, I had apprehensions and asked to go back a second time to view it. This is when I met the owner. I could not believe my eyes when I saw her, as she was an acquaintance, I had known for the last ten years or so. She owned and ran a Twice as Nice consignment store that I used to take my used clothing to. I confided in her that I was very dispirited to be on my own and told her what I was going through. She encouraged by assuring me that I would be fine and that I could do it! She too had just ended a twenty-four-year marriage and lived on the other side of the side-by-side. I felt so blessed and taken care of by the universe. We soon became friends, and life was great.

Another reason for wanting my own home was so my girls and animals could live with me comfortably. I had a cat named Clair and a Pomeranian devil of a dog that we called Meeko. The cat was originally a gift that my youngest daughter picked out from our Humane Society animal shelter.

The Pomeranian was a gift to my oldest daughter, and we both picked out and trained him. He instantly bonded with me, and we became best of friends. However, he also became very possessive and obsessed with me. My own family could not come near me without him growling at them or nipping at them. I thought, Wow! Why is this happening again? Not only did the men in my life have these traits, but now my dog! This can't be for real! There's got to be another lesson here to learn. But what?

I was so embarrassed to have people over, as he was so possessive and rowdy and would bark and nip at anyone who came too close to me. He reminded me of my first partner, who was also possessive and didn't want others around me. But I loved my Meeko so much. He was so dedicated and loved me unconditionally. I loved it when I entered the home after work or from a night out, and he was so happy to see me. We cuddled together, and I could tell him about my day, and he would listen with eagerness and no judgment. He loved to sleep beside me on the couch or under my bed and followed me around like a shadow.

CHAPTER 17

My Life in the Corporate World

"I Rejoice in My Employment
– I appreciate the opportunity to help,
Contribute to, or Serve Others.
I connect with the creativity of the universe and
allow it to flow through me in fulfilling ways.

Heart Thought Cards – Louise Hay

I thank my lucky stars and the universe for my career as an accountant. It has provided me with countless opportunities. I am so grateful to have been able to work in the private and government sectors throughout my career. I had such wonderful and pristine job opportunities throughout my working life, where I was able to use my talents and creativity to develop ways to organize and disseminate information to the public and senior management. I felt so empowered and valuable at these places.

I am so thankful for the support I had at work, people who helped me to succeed and be responsible. There were some who became good friends I could confide in and who understood where I was coming from. They kept me grounded and believed in my abilities to make a difference in this world.

I was determined to make my life meaningful, and I was hopeful for the future, even though at times the pain and emotional turmoil I was experiencing was daunting. There were times when I was so exhausted, and I wished that I didn't have to work. But I was also so thankful for my career and all the enjoyment and meaning it brought to my life. I carried on to the best of my ability and thanked the universe daily for providing all that I had.

I also loved the fact that I could be myself and had colleagues that trusted and believed in me. Even though at times, I perceived it as a rat race with a competitive edge. I enjoyed the benefits and it gave me the financial security that I needed. I also enjoyed being able to dress up in fancy clothes without fear of ridicule or judgement that I sometimes received from my family and so-called friends. I was portrayed as a fashionista which to me was a complement as I took pride in my physical appearance and loved fashion. I didn't believe I was trying to outdo anyone, just trying to fit in.

I also enjoyed the challenges and opportunities for learning new business ideas that my career gave me. I believe that these experiences gave me purpose and a passion that I might otherwise not have had. Without them, I would have perished into a deeper depression and who knows what would have come from that. But as I'll explain further on, there were many, many challenges to come.

CHAPTER 18

My Melodramatic Relationships and the Blessings Received from Them

"I get the help I need, when I need it, from various sources.
My support system is strong and loving.
– I cannot change another person.
I let others be who they are, and I simply love who I am."

Affirmation Cards - Louise Hay

What I also find to be a blessing and amazing in my life is the strong, loving relationship I have with my son. It hasn't been an easy road for us. It was very challenging to raise a healthy child from the age of sixteen, with all the dysfunction around me. And at times I felt like I was up against the world and struggled to keep him and myself safe and untethered. I felt so weak and codependent on others whom I needed in my life for support that sometimes failed to recognize his needs. I was so desperate to fulfill my emotional tank, and I felt my own selfish ways may have affected him, as I left him with his dad and other caregivers who I trusted to take care of his needs.

I've known my son's father from an early age, as he was my older brother's good friend and would hang out at our house from time to time. However, he moved away from the neighborhood, and I didn't see him or his family for a couple of years.

He came across as someone who had his life together and would be a good partner and could handle being a parent. I, being the naïve person that I was, trusted in him. To me, he was very confident in his abilities as a responsible person and parent, and I had no choice but to believe in him and forgive him for all his unhealthy addictions and control tactics.

As it turned out, my son's father (who is now deceased) was a master manipulator who inflicted some emotional and sometimes aggressive abuse on both of us. We both had to seek counselling to recover from his demeaning remarks, some of which made me believe that I was an unfit parent and unable to meet my son's needs. I always believed, and so did others, that I was a great mother and did the best that I knew how. However, I must admit that I was into my ego self and had my own selfish needs to contend with.

I met up with my son's father at a youth community center when I was thirteen years old, after returning from a trip to British Columbia, where my family was planning on moving to. We became friends and fell in love. Or should I say we had strong desires for each other, probably because of our insecurities and inability to expect anything better from others.

I soon discovered that his affection for me was not healthy and more than I could handle at the time. But because of my low self-esteem and lack of nurturing from my own invasive upbringing, I craved being loved so much and needed someone to validate my worth. I tried to overlook his jealous and possessive ways and at the time found them to be flattering! Looking back, I wish I knew then what I know now. I wish had more confidence in myself to walk away, but I was hooked.

By the time I realized how insecure he was and how codependent I would become, I was already pregnant and sixteen years old, even though I craved having my freedom more than anything. I wasn't keen on being a kept woman and endured a few blows to my already fragile self-esteem. But, despite all the negative confrontations and emotions, I still felt protected by the universe and believed things would work out.

He had an amazing family though, who I adored. I remember the first time they welcomed me to be part of their family; they took us to a Harlem Globetrotters' basketball game. It was amazing! They then invited me to other holiday functions, and I was so thrilled to be a part of his family.

When I became pregnant, I began to realize that I had to be healthy in order to have a healthy baby and to be a good mother. I quit drinking and smoking and started to eat more healthfully.

At this time in my life, I still had dreams to finish school and make something of myself, so I continued with school while I was pregnant and took a year off to care for my son while he was a baby. This wasn't the easiest thing I've had to do, but I prided myself on being a good mother. I always loved children and had already had enough experience looking after my aunts' kids while they were out either at bingo or for my other aunt who loved to ditch her kids for a few days at a time. I had to learn early on how to be responsible. I grew up fast. I always told people I was sixteen going on twenty-six at the time.

While pregnant, I thought about giving up my son for adoption because I felt that I wasn't ready to look after him full-time. I believed that it would be better for him to have two loving people than being in this family that I knew was not totally healthy. However, prior to signing the documents, my mom and his dad convinced me to keep him and promised to help me raise him. Even though I sensed that they weren't the healthiest for this, I was convinced that they were capable of helping me through this. After all, they were my only supports at the time.

When my son was born and I held him for the first time, I felt so divinely blessed and immediately filled with love and reverence. I was in awe and had faith and assurance from the universe that we could do this. I knew in my heart that it wouldn't be easy, but at the same time, I felt like I had a purpose in life to do and be more. I've never felt so much love and ambition in my life and wanted to be responsible.

For the first three years of our life, we primarily lived with my mom and went back and forth with his dad. The things that kept me well balanced through all this was taking caring of my son, going to school, and working part-time.

While living with his dad, in order to keep my stability, I decided to get a job. I got a serving job at a restaurant down the street from where we were living at the time. I worked in the evenings and enjoyed serving people. I felt so alive and empowered while I was working and out on my own.

CHAPTER 19

How the Voice of Knowledge Saved Me from Self-Destruction

"I am on an EVER CHANGING JOURNEY
– My life is never stuck or static or stale, for each moment is
New and Fresh Every ending is a new point of beginning."

Heart Thought Cards – Louise Hay

I loved going to school and thought I would just love to be a full-time student. While in high school, I took courses in accounting, typing, and biology, which of course were all my top-achieving courses. I loved biology; the anatomy of the body was so fascinating to me. This made me want to further my education in health, and I was hoping to go into the medical field after I graduated. I wanted so much to be a physician. However, since my opportunities for funding at the time were zero to none, and I didn't qualify for government funding at the time, I let this dream go. I also had many responsibilities at the time and realized that medical school wouldn't be easy. I knew I had to develop the skills I had and find something quickly to fall back on.

I loved school and what it was teaching me. However, I was in survivor mode. I decided that I was going to have to make use of the skills I had in order to succeed. I thought about what I was good at, and I decided that I could make it as an accountant, as dealing with numbers and being analytical came naturally to me. And at the time, I didn't want to deal with people or the public domain. I soon developed my résumé to support my dream of becoming an accountant.

When we moved into another home in the older west end of the city, it was an old Victorian-style house. The house was lovely but spooky. My son and I began to feel a not so welcome presence in the home. He was seeing and feeling spirits, and so was I. Of course, I had to comfort him to sleep at night and felt the same presence in his room as he had, and it was so cold.

I would ask the presence to stay away so that my son could sleep for the night, and it would go away. Of course, his dad would not believe any of this nonsense and only discounted our feelings. This bothered me so much, as I believed what my son was going through and wanted so much to comfort him so that he felt safe and secure. I too felt the presence of these spirits throughout the home, not just in his room but everywhere in the house. Our bedroom had other demons to contend with. There were also bees or wasps buzzing around the attic and around the bedroom and bathroom. Winter came, and they soon diminished, but the coldness and spirits in the home became stronger.

One day, my brother in-law brought over a psychic medium who confirmed our suspicions. She even had my son draw what he was seeing, and she too drew what she saw. They were pretty much bang on. She also advised that there was some nasty quarrelling going on in the home. She then proceeded to ask the spirits to leave. I was so relieved and thankful for her help. She also confirmed what I was feeling, as I too felt cold, eerie feelings in certain areas of the home.

I knew that I was an intuitive person and empath myself back then but didn't know how to expand on it while keeping my psychic self safe. I began to wonder what role my spirituality and faith in a higher power had to play in this. I believed in the creator and knew there were other spirits around us. I just didn't know how to deal with them readily, so I turned them away. It was so fascinating and mystical to me at the time.

My brother in-law and this psychic lady proceeded to explain incarnation and past lives. We are all part of the universal energy that uses the form of a physical body to learn and grow. She went on to explain that your spirit is born under conditions that will provide opportunities for the development of the qualities and characteristics you most need. These conditions provide you with opportunities for growth and progressive change. The framework for this change and growth is set through heredity, the time and conditions of birth (astrological and terrestrial), and environmental factors that can influence you and assist you in achieving the necessary growth.

Well, I was mesmerized by her knowledge and craved to learn more about our physiology, psychology, and connection to the universe. I went on to study, and I learned that although our life may have been predestined, we all have free will to make choices, take actions, and make decisions or not. We are not bound to fulfill what we have come to fulfill. It is true that once we have taken physical form, some factors cannot be changed. We can't change our race, genetic traits, environmental circumstances, and so forth while we are dependent on others. But once we make up our mind and develop our sixth sense by having faith and hope in that which we do not see, we can change.

Of course, being where I was at the time (not in the most stable, encouraging place) and knowing where I came from, I knew I had to work extra hard on my connections to the divine, source of all, God, and my higher power in my own way. So, to keep my faith and hope for the future on a higher vibration, I turned to horoscopes, numerology, and card readers for guidance. I knew I had to endure more lessons to become a higher-energy being with wisdom and knowledge. I began to have gratitude for what I had and focused on forgiveness and compassion for others, knowing that we are never alone in this earthly realm of the universe.

At this time, I didn't know I had psychic abilities but would feel, hear, and see apparitions that I tried to ignore. If I knew then what I know now about spirituality and mediumship, I would have welcomed these spirits into our lives. As I've learned from reading a few of Sylvia Browne's many books on her life and her success being a psychic medium, I would have been able to cope with this strange occurrence and many others.

Some of her books were fascinating and inspiring and helped me to accept this phenomenon regarding spirits, including these:

- *Adventures of a Psychic.* (She takes you through her life as a psychic and how she dealt with her gift of mediumship.)
- *The Other Side and Back—A Psychic's Guide to our World and Beyond*
- *Prophecy—What the Future Holds for You*
- *Past Lives, Future Healing—A Psychic Reveals the Secrets to Good Health and Great Relationships*

CHAPTER 20

Allowing My Ego Some Space to Heal and Grow

"I am ready to be healed. I am willing to forgive. All is well.
– I love and accept my family exactly as they are right now"

I Can Do It Cards – Louise Hay

My mental and emotional self wanted to grow and understand my spiritual self. I believed I had intuitive and psychic abilities but didn't know how to develop them. I used other forms of communicating with the divine and my higher self. I went to church, read the Bible, and believed in God as the creator and source of all that is and our connection to him through the Holy Spirit. The lack of spiritual beings in my life left me searching for spiritual wisdom and knowledge from other sources. At times, going through the depression put me on the dark side of where I wanted to be. However, I knew in my heart and soul that there would be times when magic and the divine would appear in my life with synchronistic timing.

My first intuitive card readings were from my auntie Flo. I was probably around twelve years old at the time. She was such a wonderful and wise lady and mentor in my life. She was not very educated, as I recall her telling me that she only had a grade-six education. But she had so much wisdom and positive energy that I cherished her in my life and visited her whenever I could. She loved life and all its synchronicities and taught me to believe in miracles and angels and the joy that life has to offer.

Even though she didn't have much as far as money and material goods, she had a heart of gold and loved and appreciated what she did have. She had so much wisdom and retrospection on life. She taught me that the key to having a good life is to love and accept one another. She taught me that happiness was seeing life with eyes wide open. To start each day with a happy laugh and be happy and content with what you already have. "Always do what you are afraid to do, and everything will be okay in the end. Do what feels good and believe in yourself. The best is yet to come."

She was my Louise Hay in those dark times of my life. She always encouraged me to believe in myself and my dreams. She reminded me that I deserved good in my life and to follow my dreams and not allow others to take away my possibility for success and happiness.

Doreen Virtue also teaches that in *Don't Let Anything Dull Your Sparkle*.

My aunt Flo was such a believer in divine love and God and loved hearts and angels and had them displayed throughout her home. She taught me that my guardian angels and other archangels look out for me; I only need to ask. I believe she could have written the *Heart Thought* cards by Louise Hay. Some of my favorite affirmations are these:

> I am connected with a Higher Power—The wisdom and intelligence of the Universe is mine to use. I trust in Life to support me.

> I am worth Loving—I am willing to let the love in. It is safe to Let the Love in.

> I deserve Good in my life—I am willing to go beyond my own limitations. I am wonderful, and I deserve and accept all the good that Life has to offer.

As stated, I was probably around twelve when my aunt Flo started reading my cards. She used a regular deck of cards, and I was amazed at the wonderful depictions of our life stories she could tell me or whomever she was reading for. I wanted this gift of hers and didn't realize until later in life that I have it.

She always seemed to know the answers to life's tough questions that we were seeking, even if we didn't tell her what was on our mind or going on in our lives at the time. She provided guidance surrounding a friend, a lover, a job, a new home, what the character traits of the people in my life were, or what to watch out for and what to allow into my life. Her advice was that I was free to make my own choices, to be authentic and to have boundaries, to say no if something was not the best for me, and to let it go if it was not serving my higher purpose.

When I became an adult, I started paying her for her services and bringing her customers who would give her some monetary compensation. She was one of those people who thought she shouldn't be charging for this type of work. I believed she was worth every penny and so much more.

Unfortunately, she had a disease called epilepsy that later interfered with her quality of life. She had a stroke in her late fifties and could no longer speak. She ended up in a personal care home for the last five years of her short life. I went to visit on a few occasions, and I was so heartbroken by her condition. I loved her so much, and I will always miss her, but I still feel her presence with me.

My aunt also believed, and it probably affected my programming and thinking at the time, that as a churchgoing Catholic, she should not be doing this type of divination work. She was afraid it would affect her karma. Being involved in the Christian community, I am also warned that the Bible advises against it.

However, based on the new age philosophy, I believe that being responsible requires that we consciously make our own choices, knowing that these choices will bring about certain consequences. We may hope they come out a certain way, but if we are truly responsible, we must be willing to take the consequences, whether they are good, bad, or indifferent, knowing we will learn from them. Not everything is a result of past actions, and we all create our own reality on this earthly plane.

I believe that the cards, whether regular, oracle, or tarot, are a divination tool to be used with an attitude of gratefulness, and they should be viewed as sacred. They are meant to assist you in comprehending the events, signs, and coincidences occurring in your life, and to help you recognize your dreams and aspirations. They also may activate your intuition and help you realize your purpose and potential. At least that is what they've done for me in more ways than one.

What I learned most from Aunt Flo's life and passing was that it is not unusual for many to blame everything that goes wrong in their life on bad karma. She simply confused her bad karma with poor judgment. Unfortunately, she had her own ups and downs when it came to relationships; I noticed they were not very healthy or supportive to her. Due to circumstances of living in scarcity, she did not eat the healthiest foods, and she could not kick the habit of smoking. But I do know she loved to walk, and she walked everywhere, so she was physically fit. I hope that in her next incarnation, she will find true love, health, and happiness.

I eventually found another wonderful lady mentor in my life, whose name was Madame Ruth (who is now deceased). She was another local psychic card reader. She read my cards at least every six months or so or when I had a major decision to make in my life. She used regular cards and tarot cards and taught me to follow my dreams and to believe in myself and the universe, for it would bring me guidance.

She taught me to believe in my abilities and connection to the divine and that although there may be a certain predestined outline for my life that has already been decided, it is being influenced by my environment and circumstances, and that is a result of the past and my upbringing.

She encouraged me to develop new abilities and to work on my creativity and intuition. She was very inspiring and taught me to make my life into an adventure and to take the unknown and embrace it like my own. She challenged me to be a light worker in the world, which I really had to work on and still do.

I always left the card readings feeling empowered and determined to make the right choices, as tedious as they might have been at the time. I wanted my life to be normal and for everything around me to be beautiful and safe. I searched for divine guidance, and the choices I made most times worked out for the highest good for all those involved in and around my life. I started doing my own card readings after her passing and am finally coming out of the spiritual closet so that I too can assist people in realizing what our divine life has to offer.

Besides seeking advice from psychic card readers, I also found a few psychic mediums who gave me readings and let me know that I have guardian angels, spirit guides, and ancestors with me all the time. They advise that these spirits are here to assist me on my spiritual journey and ensure my safety, and they will provide assistance to me whenever I request it.

I am so grateful to have found spiritual teachers who have provided me with the guidance needed for my awakening to the power of the divine, universal energy, and source of all that is, God.

CHAPTER 21

Other Dragons to Tame

"I am Safe and Secure in my World –
If I have a compulsive habit, I realize that there is some need in
my consciousness for this condition or it would not be there."

Wisdom Cards – Louise Hay

When I was in my early twenties, I tried to make a go of it with my son's father, and to keep my stability, I found a job as a receptionist at an accounting firm. It was my first real job, and I loved working there, doing the bookkeeping, typing up corporate returns, answering calls, and so on. Unfortunately, I was laid off after working there for six months, but I knew that was all the experience I needed to get my next job. It was just a stepping-stone, as the saying goes.

Soon after I was laid off, I could no longer take the manipulation and the and ups and downs of life's struggles. I knew I had to become stronger to survive on my own. My soul was crying out for healing and understanding, but my ego wanted to maintain power.

I found a place of my own in a subsidized housing block and went to school. My brother lived with me temporarily and was a great help with my son and the chores around the house. Luckily, he loved to cook, while I studied. We took turns at it and really learned from each other.

Unfortunately, my brother and my son's father did not see eye to eye about something or another and had a fist fight in my apartment and damaged the wall. I was so disappointed, but I couldn't blame anyone and just asked them to grow up for my son's sake, and life went on. All I wanted was a normal life and some peace and stability, minus the drama.

I realized that I was still not emotionally strong enough to make it on my own. I kept moving in and out of this relationship with my son's father. My ego had this need for something outside of myself that made me feel so insignificant that I started to believe I might not be able to make a go of this life. I started to believe in the negative portrayal he had of me. I knew if I didn't get out of that relationship, I would become a statistic of domestic abuse. I didn't want to be a victim or live as a martyr.

It was extremely difficult to leave without a support system and with a damaged ego. However, I still had my faith, hope, and divine spiritual self that needed to heal. I picked myself up and decided to finish my schooling and worked part-time while co-parenting with this oppressor.

I never wanted my son to know how his dad's behavior affected me and never did tell him all the details. I hope that if he reads this, he can learn to forgive his dad as I have forgiven him. Although my son is doing great now and I am so proud of him, I believe we both may have had a negative impact on his outlook on life, and I only hope he has forgiven us and become strong and remain healthy.

Because I wanted so much to have peace between us, I would remain friends with this person, for the sake of our son and because he made me believe that he was the better parent. Because of my own insecurities and need to improve my life, I believed him. I found out later from my son that he was very abusive to him too. I felt so guilty and horrible for this too. I hope my son has forgiven me and his dad for this.

As I attended school and worked on getting my life together, my son's dad had guardianship of him and was involved in a relationship with a very nice person to whom I am forever grateful for being a positive influence in my son's life. Life became a little easier, and my faith in miracles was restored.

CHAPTER 22

Reminiscing About the Good Old Days

"There is a Solution to Every Problem.
– We create habits and problems to fulfill a need. When I can
find a positive way to fulfill the need, I can release the problem."

Wisdom Cards – Louise Hay

When I was around twenty-six, I was working at the head office of a fashion designer/manufacture as a junior accountant. I was single, had a nice little red sports car, and was living with my mom. Life was magical. I say that because prior to being hired at this business, I was in a position at another clothing manufacturing company and was working twelve- to fourteen-hour days and feeling a bit burned out. A friend of mine, an accountant who I met working part-time at a boat excursion business, wrote me a letter of offer to work at the head office of this business. I was ecstatic and relieved, and I believed that my needs had been divinely answered. I was so thankful.

Around the same time, my son's dad allowed me to have my son back in my life, to live with me. I was so excited but knew that I could not keep him in my mother's two-bedroom suite. The next day, I went to the subsidized housing office and was offered a beautiful two-bedroom apartment/ townhouse in a wonderful neighborhood, where I could feel safe and secure. It also happened to be situated only a few blocks away from where his dad was living and closer to where I was working.

I felt so blessed that fate was finally on my side. My son and I could finally have a life together. We were both happy and grateful for where we were. At the time, I thought I was living on top of the world. I know now that "loving myself and thinking joyful, happy thoughts was the quickest way to create a wonderful life," as Louise Hay and Dr. Wayne Dyer taught me.

Unfortunately, the guy I had dated for the last five years had other plans for us and wasn't impressed that I had other responsibilities to consider. He started to become rude and insulting toward me, so I called it quits with him. Even though he was a very nice guy and we had great times together, I felt it was best to go our separate ways.

Soon after we split up, I met another young man at a nightclub where I was out with one of my girlfriends to relax and dance a bit. I was being hit on by a belligerent person, and I noticed this other young man standing close by, so I asked if we could just talk and act like we were friends. I didn't expect anything to come of it, as he was very young looking. I thought he was in his early twenties, but he was sober, which was a relief. I was twenty-six at the time and not looking for a complicated relationship. However, he asked for my phone number, and I gave it to him, not expecting him to call anytime soon.

He called the following weekend and asked if I would like to go camping with him and his buddies. I laughed and said I didn't think so. We ended up going out the following weekend to his friend's home who lived on a houseboat, boarded at a yacht club. This was another great time in my life. I met a new group of friends and felt so lucky to be alive, although I was always a bit nervous and had an anxious feeling in my solar plexus.

He came across as a responsible guy with no inhibitions. However, about two months into our relationship, I found out he had a child of his own that I would become the stand-in caregiver to. I grew to love his son as my own, and even my son loved him. I felt like I had a new functional, blended family. Life was good.

I trusted our future together, and we decided to buy a home together in the country. I always wanted to live in the country, although my expectation was within three kilometers of the city, but I did not voice this with clarity. I soon realized what he wanted and what I wanted did not match up. He ended up finding us a home forty kilometers out of the city limits and fifty kilometers from where I worked, which was downtown in the city we were from.

Although I wasn't crazy about the fact that he chose the home and sealed the deal without me seeing it first, I did learn to love it, as it was another one of my dreams. It was gorgeous, with tons of windows all around and facing south. I enjoyed decorating and making it our home.

Mind you, I wasn't expecting a home in the middle of nowhere with forty acres of land, three acres of yard space with grass to mow, rocks and forest, and a few gravel roads to travel on to get there. I did love being in the country though and in nature; it was so peaceful and calming. I believe my kids also loved it, and they are nature lovers to this day.

Soon after we moved in together, our life became a constant ordeal to survive, especially when I realized that we had only a woodburning furnace. We had to purchase wood and had to constantly feed the furnace throughout our first winter there, from morning till night. I was so grateful that my son was with us to help. He was so helpful, getting up early after my husband left for work and putting more wood in the fire. He also helped cut and pile the wood and haul it into the house daily.

Although we wanted to and planned on having more children in the future, I became pregnant sooner than expected and realized it was not going to be an easy road ahead. After giving birth to my daughter, I was excited but a little disheartened by the lack of support I had available. I did my best to stay positive.

My cortisol instinct was to run back to the city, but at the time, I was too exhausted, as I was working full-time and soon became pregnant with our second daughter. I continued to operate our household the best way I knew how, most times conflicting with his need to be in control of the finances, which did not mesh well with me. I was too used to being independent and knew how to run a household. After all, I had been pretty much self-reliant and on my own since I was fifteen.

I found that the more I spent on things that I felt were necessary for the home or family without consulting him first, the more we argued and disagreed. I found this extremely intimidating and difficult to understand at the time. After all, I was also earning money and didn't believe I had to check in with him. I considered myself a responsible adult who could manage the finances and the kids' needs, all while working full-time and dealing with chronic fatigue. To say the least, I was a little frazzled most days. I soon became self-absorbed and chose not to share what I spent our money on and didn't allow it to be a joint effort.

He was so busy running a business at the time and did not get home until late into the evening. We also did not communicate well when we were both so exhausted from work. Most times when I called him at work, we would get upset with each other and leave me distraught and in tears. I was very confused and disturbed by these behaviors and my fear of abandonment.

There were times when we would argue so wildly, I would end up in tears of frustration. I was worried about how this was affecting our kids' well-being. I later found out that our arguments scared them, but they appeared unshaken.

He also hated it if I used any type of credit, even when there were times where I needed to buy things that I believed to be necessities. I was used to buying on credit, and I had no doubts that it could be paid off. Out of fear for our financial future, he would take my credit and debit cards and destroy them. Although this took my power away, I accepted that it was just another tactic to show his control and contribution to our household.

What I learned from this was that no matter how frazzled and powerless I felt at the time, there were certain things that were working in my life. I had a wonderful job and beautiful children. I had a beautiful home and neighbors that became my friends. Despite the depression and chronic fatigue, I was able to stay active for my kids, as they gave me a purpose to live for.

I was resourceful and creative at making our home a beautiful haven and sanctuary. I still believed that life should be joyous, as we all strive for bliss, peace, love, health, and freedom, and most times we have these.

I must thank my coworkers, my newfound neighbor friends, and my in-law(s) who were all so very supportive of me and got me through those times unscathed and resilient. I am especially grateful to my kids and my ex-husband for bringing me joy and harmony when times were good.

CHAPTER 23

Fond Memories Working Out My Karma

"I rise above my limitations
– Whenever I encounter a challenge in my life,
I use the experience to learn and grow.

Wisdom Cards – Louise Hay

My son was a wonderful kid. He was so friendly and outgoing and had such a positive outlook on life. He loved to do things and help wherever and whoever he could. He was so helpful and independent, and I was so proud of him. Besides the chore of keeping the furnace stoked, he would help me with the laundry and keeping his room tidy.

He also loved participating in cooking and baking in our beautiful chef's kitchen. We would make all kinds of meals together. There was a time we made pumpkin pie from scratch. I guess I forgot to strain the cooked pumpkin mixture before putting it into the pie crust, and it did not want to cook. I was ready to throw it out. Well, he suggested that we strain the pumpkin and try again. It turned out to be such a delicious pie.

I have so many good memories of this home and my blended family with all the fervor of living—or shall I say surviving. This was when I realized that I was a city girl and needed to become more resourceful and robust for this country living.

Well, I could tell that I had many more lessons to learn before I could be healed and connect to my higher self. I learned this in a course I took with Sara Wiseman, "Releasing Yourself from Family Karma":

> Every family—including mine had its challenges, its secrets, its failings, its shadows. In most cases, these karmic challenges center around seven key issues:
>
> Abuse
> Addiction
> Violence
> Poverty
> Illness
> Abandonment
> Betrayal

Believe me—my blended diverse family and many other families I grew up with had it all. In fact, every family I have ever known had some of these behaviors. Both my partner and I already knew that we were from broken families, which on hindsight is probably why we came together. We had lessons to learn from each other.

Around the same time that we decided to cohabitate and move to our gorgeous home in the country, my partner and his brother were offered the opportunity to run a service station on the other side of the city, around seventy kilometers away. Although I was excited for them, I knew in my heart that it was not going to be a smooth ride. The irony was that it was a result of a proposal that I helped them write.

I loved being in the country; if only I didn't need the job in the city. I loved being in nature and felt so connected to spirit while being out there.

But I also felt isolated and abandoned. I really wanted to be in the city, close to our families, as I needed their support. After a couple of months of being in our new home, I became pregnant, and life became even more stressful. I felt even more alone and trapped all over again. At the same time, I was excited and felt that I had a purpose in my life to strive for. My children became my foundation and passion for life.

About a year before we moved to the country, I started a wonderful career with the federal public sector. I was so grateful to have this job, as it was such a blessing to be able to use my accounting background in creative ways, developing spreadsheets and doing financial analysis that I felt I was born to do.

Even when the union decided to go on strike, I felt that there was no need for it, as I was content where I was and what I was doing. However, overall, the morale of others did improve afterward. Because I was pregnant with our second daughter and needed to put in the time, I could cross the picket line as long as I went out on my breaks.

I returned to work immediately after my benefits ran out, which I believe was six months back then. Most times, it was an accomplishment and feat to get my toddlers ready every morning and drive them to the sitter, and I was exhausted by the time I got to work. But I believe my job contributed to my sanity, as I didn't feel so isolated, and it gave me purpose to go on.

It is amazing how older siblings want to be a help and look after and out for their siblings, including myself. My oldest daughter did whatever she could to console or help her sister with whatever we were doing, whether reprimanding her for not moving fast enough or helping her get dressed. I had to remind her that I was the mother and she should only help when asked to. I always believed that children should be empowered to be responsible for themselves and assist others when necessary.

I remember the first time my oldest daughter amazed me with her ability to nurture her sister. She must have been less than two years old, as they are seventeen months apart. Her sister was fussing, as it was feeding time. I went to the kitchen to warm up her bottle and asked her to stay by her side. She said, "Sure, Mommy. I will watch over her and keep her quiet"—in her own baby language, that is. I returned a minute or so later and found her with one thumb in her mouth and the other in her sister's, holding onto her blankie as usual. It was such a precious and charming moment; it still brings tears to my eyes and a picture to my mind that I will never forget.

When we first moved out to our spectacular country home, my son was a fundamental part of our life. He was so helpful at times, but like most kids needed some discipline and boundaries. I guess because of the pressures of work life and home, my partner and I were both under a lot of stress and argued and disagreed on a lot of stuff. We could not agree on how to discipline our children, which brought on a lot of frustration for both of us.

Prior to becoming more informed and educated about disciplining children, most people in my family tried to convince me that using force and bullying was the way to discipline a child, so they could learn how to respect you. I wouldn't buy into this. I did not believe in emotional or physical punishment of any kind and would not tolerate it in my household.

I learned other techniques from reading books and going to workshops on how to get along with and discipline our kids. My favorites are *How to Talk so Kids Will Listen, How to Listen so Kids Will Talk,* and Barbara Coloroso's *Kids Are Worth It* and her *Parenting with Wit and Wisdom in Times of Chaos and Loss.*

Unfortunately, around this time, I became exhausted from dealing with my postpartum depression and chronic fatigue syndrome and thought it was best for my son to go live with his biological father.

Like most families, I could sense that my partner was also a victim of family karmic shadows. Despite this, I felt we had a soul connection, and I had compassion and empathy for him. He became another purpose in my life and I was his. I felt we could build each other up and fill our own egoic and spiritual needs together. We became inter dependent and relied on each other for validation of our existence.

I admired his tenacity for life and his dedication to our marriage and family. Although we both felt like the martyr in our relationship, we did respect and love each other enough to allow the other room to breathe and grow spiritually. Even though I believed that this life was beautiful and better than my last, I felt that our lives could be better.

Looking back, I see that I let my power go by allowing negativity to cloud my intuitive judgment that life was for me and not against me. I vowed to view others in a more spiritual light and decided that energy/emotional vampires would no longer affect my being as they once had.

CHAPTER 24

Dealing with Karmic Debris and the Need for Forgiveness and Love

"I nurture my inner child –
Loving your inner child helps you remember your
innocence and recognize how much Life Love You."
"Ask the child within "What can I do for you today?"

Life Loves You Cards – Louise Hay and Robert Holden

It took many years of counselling and soul searching to forgive myself for letting my son go live with his dad again. But I felt so trapped at that time in my life while trying to make it in the country with two babies to care for. I didn't have the confidence or patience to be a good enough parent. I did believe strongly though that although we were apart from each other, I always had and will have a heart connection to him.

This has taught me that karma can present itself in unpleasant ways and that anything you do provides opportunity for change and growth, whether it is something from the past or something happening now. We each learn our lessons differently because we are each at our own level of spiritual growth.

The consequences will vary from individual to individual. Mine was to endure and accept myself and others' imperfections. To work on my inner self, my spirituality and connection to the divine, while loving myself and forgiving those close to me, including myself.

Within one's life lessons, there can be many variations and many life situations that provide the best opportunity for learning and acquiring wisdom. If there has been a misuse of a person's free will, circumstances will unfold so that the soul can learn to use it productively. I had to learn to forgive those who unintentionally harmed me and go on with being the best version of light and love I could possibly be. I've known the following on a soul level, and it has been confirmed by Ana Holub in the course Heal Addictions with Forgiveness:

> In order to rebuild our lives, we must be blazingly honest. It's time to admit that when we crave, we crave inner peace. And to directly experience this peace, we need to change direction, leaving all illusions and cover-ups behind.

> Our souls cry out for healing and understanding, but our egos want to maintain power. The ego's sole mission is to keep us feeling separated, lonely, and

desperate - the very last thing an ego wants us to experience is forgiveness. It feels threatened to its very core. Its response is to manipulate, threaten and attack us and others, so that it can remain intact and live another day.

This makes so much sense to me now, as my addictions to not only substances but activities were a divining rod for difficulty, challenge, and pain that I was experiencing at the time. My addiction to romantical love and my need for validation were interfering with my connection to others, especially my family and partners.

Along with balance in the rest of your life (nutrition, exercise, socializing with high-vibe people, nature time, reprioritizing, being creative, etc.), you must include forgiving yourself and others if you want to expand into something new, amazing, enlivening, and very different than being an addict or a victim to life's circumstances.

No one can do this for you. Fortunately, it's your free-will choice.

As I previously mentioned, I hope that I can redeem myself my children, family, friends and ex-partners whose chaos I contributed to back then. May they forgive me as I learn to forgive myself with love and compassion.

I also learned that my extreme sensitivity and being an empath has provided me with the love and compassion for myself and others, to want to make a difference in their lives as best I could.

I'm beginning to realize that the most important principle in creating a well-balanced spiritual life is to have and be love. It is important to know that a relationship is not the only source of love. Love doesn't come from the outside. Love comes from within.

I am learning this even more while I study Barbara De Angelis's online course:

> Secrets for Living the Life You Want will help you find true freedom—the freedom to reconnect with the power of love in your heart, to push past the walls and protections, and to dissolve the blocks so love can

flow more fully into all your relationships and bring you true intimacy and fulfillment. It will give you the freedom to stop making the same mistakes or getting stuck in the same places. And you'll emerge with the freedom to express the whole, magnificent you, and to live with new confidence, clarity, and genuine peace.

Thank you again to Hay House and other spiritual authors for the books and courses that I needed in my life. They have inspired me to become a more robust and spiritual human being while giving me the hope and encouragement I need to continue my sacred journey to health and wellness.

CHAPTER 25

Life Lessons Learned from My Spiritual Teachers

"I am open and receptive to love
– Life is always trying to love you, but you need to
be Open to see it. Complete this sentence: I could
make it Easier for Life to Love me by…"

Life Loves You Cards – Louise Hay and Robert Holden

As taught to me by many spiritual teachers, the soul does not have to suffer to progress. Suffering is only good for the soul if it teaches us how not to suffer again. Although it seemed so at the time, I knew in my soul that progress will only occur if I live in harmony with the natural laws of the universe. If you have been out of harmony, which I have been, and work to bring yourself back into harmony with your soul connections, karma can be constructive, with its aim as guidance. It teaches us that we cannot separate ourselves from others who are here to teach us lessons in life.

It appeared that most of my life had struggles and misfortunes. They say that fibro is caused by traumatic events in one's life. When I think back on my experiences, I had many, many unpleasant and traumatic events that I am sure contributed to this debilitating and annoying disease called fibromyalgia. But I wasn't going to let it define me.

In hindsight, in my twenties, I was so exhausted and uneasy most of the time, especially when I got home from work. As much as I loved work and using my skills in creative ways was very self-affirming, I still had my own insecurities to deal with. I was always exhausted from all the roles and changes happening in my life and the workplace. Trying to make it in a man's world was also an issue that I had to come to terms with. I knew I had to keep educating myself in order to compete for better jobs.

I realized that working full-time, taking care of a family from a very young age, doing all the grocery and other shopping, preparing lunches and dinners every day, and performing all household chores can, after a while, wear on a person. I considered myself a super mom. I wore many hats—mother, housewife, chef, chauffer, family counsellor, and professional accountant.

I earned my certificate in advanced accounting while studying and attending lectures once a week at the University of Manitoba. My young children at the time were so patient but also a little disappointed that I had to study so much. My son would often ask why I had to study and why I couldn't just be a stay-at-home mom and bake cookies like most moms did. My daughters begged me to spend more time with them. I was torn between two worlds. I needed to find balance.

After around ten years of studying part-time, working, and raising my family, I finally made it to the national exams and aspired to become a certified management accountant. I was so proud of myself and so excited to take the exam. Well, I wrote the four-hour intensive exam on day one and thought I did a great job; I became ill at the end of the first day's exam. I did make it to day two of the eight-hour exam, but unfortunately did not pass.

Repeating this ordeal meant I would have had to study for another six months prior to writing the next exam the following year. At the time, I was emotionally and physically exhausted with no outside support.

On the positive side, I was given time off at my job to pursue my dream of obtaining this certification. I had to study and be home with my children all day, and then had to hire a sitter while I went to class in the evenings. I was riddled with guilt and exhaustion, and this was just too much for me to endure. I felt alone and defeated, so I gave it up.

I decided I wasn't going to be an accountant anymore, and I found another job opportunity as a statistical analyst for the province. It was fascinating working with the humongous database of information. I was tasked with manipulating the medical and pharmaceutical data and providing reports that were used to make sense of why our population was so dependent and reliant on our medical and pharmaceutical options. And why were these costing our taxpayers so much year after year?

After doing this for a year or so, other divisions found out that I had a financial background, and I was pulled back into the arena of the finance world of budgets and analysis. It was challenging at times, but I loved it.

Even though I couldn't use the initials CPA, CMA, or PhD, I did receive a certification in advanced accounting from the University of Manitoba. I considered myself qualified, and most of my colleagues and bosses considered me a professional accountant anyway. I believed that I was qualified, and I was determined to stay in the profession. I considered myself a professional and took my career and business life seriously. I prided myself as a WIP (work in progress) and survivor of life.

I was not going to let the failure of not receiving the CMA designation prevent my future dreams and aspirations. I just decided that I was competent enough and capable enough to develop my skills as required in any position I found myself in. I thank the universe for all the wonderful job opportunities I was given in my career as an accountant—from my first real office job as an accounts receivable/computer operator to my most recent accounting positions as a financial / business analyst. I enjoyed and took pride in them all. I am truly grateful for all the experiences I've been given.

Despite my successes, I was still in pain, both emotionally and physically. I went to physicians and counselors many times, trying to find a solution for my chronic fatigue and depression. I believe it started out as chronic fatigue syndrome, but I didn't receive confirmation of this from my physician. With this and other ailments, I just kept living the best I could. When you have a plethora of responsibilities to family and home, you just do the best you can with what you have. Even though I was weary and depressed, I wasn't going to let it define who I wanted to be. I still loved life and all its magical moments and synchronicities.

I always believed that my life was soon going to be filled with the health and prosperity that I am destined to fulfill. My mission in life is to serve others so that they may find theirs too.

CHAPTER 26

Coming to Know and Believing in a Higher Power and My Soul Growth

"I release the past with ease, and I trust the process of life
– I do not use yesterday's mental garbage to create tomorrow's
experiences. I create fresh new thought and a fresh new life."

Wisdom Cards – Louise Hay

My soul journey started when I was around three or four years old. We were either at our home or a relative's home in the oldest part of our city. We were in the backyard of a home, and I fell into a dark hole under the deck. In that place, I felt like I was in hell. I literally came face-to-face with a couple of demons with a fire in the background. I was mesmerized but not afraid.

I believe now that these demons were perhaps spirits of some kind trying to warn of the hazards surrounding me at the time. It wasn't the poshest of neighborhoods, but this was where we lived, and life was magical. There were also a lot of festivities and things going on around me. Looking back, I believe those beings that I saw, although they weren't the best-looking creatures, were my guardian angel and spirit guides, merely trying to console me. Thinking back, I don't know if it was real or a dream, it was as life could be at times an illusion. I don't even know how I got out of that hole, but I did, unscathed but a bit shaken.

Because of my belief in guardian angels and spirit guides, I also had a strong faith in Jesus and angels, so much so that at age four, my brothers asked me to go up in the attic to stake out our Christmas presents. I went up reluctantly, carrying a huge cross with Jesus on it. It was a beautiful rendition of him. I went up in the dark with a flashlight, found the light switch, and noticed a box full of our gifts still unwrapped. However, I was so fearful that I can't remember what the presents were to this day.

Irrespective of believing in angels, Jesus, and of course God, our creator of all, including our source energy and the power greater than ourselves, I never bought into the doctrine of the Catholic Church. Most of my family professes to be Catholic and brags about attending catechism. Despite their confessions of being Roman Catholic, I've observed and found humorous their beliefs in superstitious sacraments and rituals to ensure blessings or protection and using sacred signs to ensure well-being or luck. I, on the other hand, have come to believe in these also, as crystals and oracle cards are my way to ensure light energy surrounds me.

Although I believed my mother to be godly, intuitive, and psychic,

I still think it's cute that she worries about the future so much—and I mean always.

I recently found this on a daily blog that I follow, and I immediately shared it with my mother. It is from Madison Taylor of the Daily OM:

> Worry is an extension of fear and can also set you up for attracting that which you don't want in your life.
>
> As caring individuals, we all worry about something and someone at various times in our lives. However, some of us have a habitual tendency to worry, and all of us have known someone who is a chronic worrier. Worry is an extension of fear and can be a very draining experience. In order for worry to exist, we have to imagine that something bad might happen. What we are worrying about has not happened yet, however, so this bad thing is by definition imaginary. Understood this way, worry is a self-created state of needless fear. Still, most of us worry.

Fear, on the other hand, is defined as false events appearing real. Another reasons we worry is that we are avoiding something that is nagging us, such as unpaid bills, debt, or scarcity of basic needs and resources.

I really try to surrender to my worries, so I am not leading an anxiety-driven life based on fear of the unknown. I've been advised and believe worry is wasting our life energy on future events, as we cannot change the fate of others by doing so. Worrying is using your imagination to create something you don't want.

I've been told by a few of my friends and acquaintances that I'm a resourceful person, and I didn't quite know what that meant until now. It's because I always believed that the universe and God were there for me and would always take care of my needs. Believe me— there were times when I was almost homeless, and the universe came through for me. Thank you, thank you, thank you.

Like me, my mother loved having her cards read by my wonderful clairvoyant aunt Flo, who was a very psychic card reader. She read our past, present, and future events with love and compassion. However, at times, she did advise us of not so good things to come, which I'm sure only added to my mother's fears and worries.

My mother also believes in many of the self-declared psychics and clairvoyants who have been sending her letters telling her that she will win or receive some big money or inheritance someday! I am talking about people from other countries such as Hong Kong, Spain, the Netherlands, France, Switzerland, and Australia. I can't believe they can get away with these false promises. But she will only receive the "blessings," they advise, if she responds and sends them the money needed to process these claims.

It is also sad that they make her believe in curses and sorcery that could bring harm to her if she doesn't heed their advice. The reason I know this is because she's allowed me to read some of these letters, although she's been advised not to talk to anyone about them. I really try hard to tell her that these people are professional con artists and fraudulent. I've tried to block the letters by sending them back to the sender, to no avail.

Despite trying to have her name taken off these mailing lists and informing antifraud authorities, I gave up. I just hope that she's more in tune with her own prosperity and doesn't give into their scamming ways to allow them to pilfer money from her as they did in the past. I still can't believe what these people from other countries can get away with and the stories they make up. I guess this is what the evils of bad marketing is meant to deliver. I've read so many stories of older people being scammed of their life savings, and I hope this doesn't happen to anyone else.

Most people growing up in our so-called tough and turbulent neighborhood, including my relatives, had such ingenuous vocabulary of despicable words that it would make me cringe at times. Whenever someone crossed them or made them angry or something didn't go their way, they would curse vulgarities and always have someone to blame for their misery.

Maybe I've become accustomed to it, but they and my mom are not so vulgar these days. However, she is still apt to curse others, including me, if she doesn't agree with the way things are and when she is a bit cranky. I wish she would be less dramatic and accepting of people. I also wish that she would be less negative about her impoverished life and take responsibility for her treasures and misfortunes.

When I was younger, I was never allowed to express my true feelings to my mother or any other person in her presence. I was usually reprimanded or ill advised, so I never spoke up, for fear of being yelled at or smacked. I understand that raising seven rambunctious kids was a bit overwhelming and may have contributed to our severe punishments at times, and I have forgiven her for this. I also forgive my sister and brothers who may have contributed to our punishments, as we were always squabbling over something or other.

We are very fortunate to have a child protection branch and provincial laws that protect our most vulnerable children and elders against physical and emotional abuse. I know of situations where neglect and mistreatment happened within our family of origin. A few of our other family members had their children taken away for mistreating or neglecting them. Unfortunately, my mother and I had to make the call a few times on behalf of my cousins when I observed them being neglected and feared for their safety.

I remember the last time my mother was going to inflict physical force on me. She came at me with a broom. I was around twelve years old then and wouldn't jump to do the dishes. I had started to become a bit rebellious, and I wasn't going to get a beating for such a menial task. I had also just come in from playing baseball or some other sport and was a bit tired and crabby. I grabbed the broom and swung her to the ground, not with the intention of wrestling with her; I was just defending myself. I just didn't want to get another unnecessary beating. I didn't mean it disrespectfully but had to let her know that I wasn't going to tolerate it any longer.

I was so perceptive when I was a child that people would comment that I was angelic and that I could help them with their life's lessons.

I remember being very inquisitive as a child and knowing almost at a genius level answers to life's dilemmas, or so I thought. And then I started to develop my own knowledge of the world. I believe we all start out this way, and then, while growing up, we are programmed by our well-meaning elders that life is not so easy and predictable, and we must follow their ways.

These thoughts were verified after reading *The Voice of Knowledge* by Don Miguel Ruiz, *A Practical Guide to Inner Peace*. I've also read his book *The Four Agreements* and am in the process of reading his other book in this Wisdom of Life series, *The Mastery of Love*.

When I was older and more independently minded, there was a time when I wanted nothing to do with my family, including my mom and dad. I wouldn't talk to them for months at a time. As I came to know about karma, I realized that you cannot just walk away and expect to forget until you have forgiven. You must give of yourself and love them unconditionally at a soul level, as that is what we are here to do. It is our dharma; I am led to believe. I supposedly chose this family to learn some lessons in this lifetime. Believe me—I still question myself as to why.

Of the six siblings I had in my family, my oldest brother and I are the only ones still alive. I had a brother who took his life when he was twenty-one. I was nineteen. That was probably one of the first real tragedies in my life, as I was very close to him. I felt completely lost and betrayed by it. After the grieving, I considered him to be my guardian angel or spirit guide from then on. I also learned to trust in my angels and spirit guides and always felt their presence with me.

My third oldest brother passed away from heart disease at age fifty-four, and even though he did some unpleasant things to my sister, I forgive him. Despite his immoral trespasses, I believe he had a good heart and soul. He had his own demons to conquer. I hope his soul has grown and he is at peace on the other side.

His passing was such a tragedy and especially sad for the beautiful daughter he left behind. My niece is an amazing person and the mother of two beautiful daughters and a very spirited son. I truly hope they are divinely led, as I am, to become whole and healthy.

My younger sister perished of alcoholism at the young age of forty-nine. I was again heartbroken. While she was alive, I attempted to create a bond between us and begged her to stop drinking. She would stop for a few months at a time and was such a beautiful person when she was sober. Unfortunately, I believe she wouldn't let go of the past and had resentments toward our family and others for mistreating her in her earlier years. I know this because she would call me while under the influence of drugs or alcohol and tell me about her perceptions of the past. I often asked her to forgive and move on, but she wouldn't let go. I admit that I did let her down for various reasons and asked her for forgiveness many times. I hope she has forgiven me, as I have forgiven myself for treating her unkindly at times.

It is so sad to say that our families felt relieved when she passed because of the worry and turmoil she put us through. There were so many times I'd get a call in the middle of the night from my mother, begging me to go out and find her on the streets of downtown Winnipeg. I halfheartedly tried at times and later realized that this was her doing and we couldn't save her from her mayhem. What a loss of another good soul.

My second oldest brother passed away of diabetes complications at age sixty in Vancouver, BC. He too had a rough life, living as a homeless person most of his adult life while suffering from mental disorders. He was another sad story in my life and unfortunately caused a lot of grief to me, my sister, and our family. However, I still love him and forgive him for all his trespasses and hope he is at peace on the other side.

To this day, I do try my best to assist my mother and brother as they gracefully age, especially since neither of them drive. I also have power of attorney for my mom, due to our joint bank account where we share responsibility for the mortgage on her home.

Even though my mother won a lottery back in 2005 and received a substantial amount of money, it didn't last long. By the end of 2011, the money was all used up. She became addicted to gambling and was conned by unsolicited advisers that she would inherit money from afar. Her common-law husband was an alcoholic and became chronically ill with COPD. He was in and out of the hospital and finally transitioned to a personal care home and passed away the following year.

He took out a mortgage that she denies agreeing to, although her signature is on the documents, so she refused to pay for it after his passing. She believes that he committed fraud and forged her name on the mortgage documents. I searched her bank accounts and found that they both had a turn in spending these funds. The money was needed to pay down debt and replenish the bank account, as they both became too reliant on the credit that was available to them at the time.

Unfortunately, we did not have the funds to pay a lawyer to fight this transgression, and it was kind of pointless since the transgressor was deceased. I advised her that if she didn't keep up the payments, the bank would take her home away. A few months later, just as I feared, my mom's home was seized, and she and my brother became homeless.

I didn't need this drama or responsibility, as I was planning on retiring that year. However, even though I was reluctant, I felt so bad for her and my brother that I decided to help her refinance so that she could get her home back. The mortgage and line of credit is now in both of our names. To this day, I am not at ease with this decision and only hope it can be dissolved.

Most times, my brother and she manage financially but still struggle to make ends meet. Despite all this, they consider me their financial restitution, and I still need to save them financially when funds are short and addictions and chronic pain reveal themselves. If it weren't for their smoking and drug addictions, I believe they could manage financially.

Although their needs are demanding at times and I do feel overwhelmed at times, my hope is that they will someday see the glimmer of hope and power of the universe to assist them, which ironically appears to be me. If only they could realize the divine presence in the synchronicities of our challenges. My family has never been on the positive aspects of life page and have only known life to be a struggle.

I, on the other hand, always believed that I could do better with my life, if only I could become more educated, empowered, and confident in myself and my abilities. And of course, I wanted to be spiritually led, as I am a free spirit and know I have guardian angels and guides on my side. I knew from a young age that the power of the universe is there to help us succeed in life, and so it is.

CHAPTER 27

My Life Back in the Days of Darkness

"I now Go Beyond other Peoples Fears and Limitations
– It is my mind that creates my experiences. I am unlimited
in my own ability to create the good in my Life."

Power Thought Cards – Louise Hay

I wholeheartedly believe that what threw me off the path of my divinity were portrayals of life on television back in the day, the chiller thrillers that were on TV starting in the black-and-white era. When I was a toddler, I watched the movie *King Kong* and other dinosaur movies and was so freaked out that I was afraid to sleep at night. Then there was the *Twilight Zone* and the *Outer Limit* series of short stories. I was a bit older when I started watching those and found them quite fascinating, but due to my wild imagination and sensitivity, I was deeply affected by them. In fact, I was so distraught at the reality of the illusion of my life that I didn't know what was real or not back then, especially being influenced by what I was watching on television.

Other events that contributed to the drama and traumas in my life happened when I was out wandering about on my own. I was probably only four or five at the time, and for some reason, someone started chasing me and pushed me, and I fell on some glass and cut open my wrist. I had to go to the emergency room and get stitches, not a great experience for a young child. I still remember the nurses holding me down while I had to get the stitches. I still have the scar on my wrist and was lucky that it did not sever any major arteries, as it was pretty close to them.

I was also cursed, so I believed, by my aunt who was living with us at the time. While she was at school, being the curious, creative explorer that I was, I went through some of her things and found some art supplies. And being the creative genius, I was at the time, I had a great time with them. Well, she got so upset that she alleged something bad would happen to me. Soon after that, I stepped on a nail and ended up in the hospital again for stitches. It was another traumatic experience that I endured at the hands of not so encouraging nurses and doctors, or so I thought.

One day there was a disturbing incident while I was walking to the corner store. A guy pulled up and offered me some money or candy; I don't quite recall what it was. I was probably around seven or eight at the time. Well, being the happy-go-lucky kid that I was, I said sure, and as I walked up to the vehicle, I noticed he had no clothes on. Well, I panicked and frantically ran home as fast as I could.

I ran to my mom and dad, crying hysterically. To my astonishment, they both reamed me out for approaching the guy! I felt like they were blaming me for the incident, and I felt so guilty and berated that I no longer confided in my mother any future incidents, for fear of her response.

The irony of it is that I soon found out that the guy was a friend of my dad's, and I was unable to tell him. I was so terrified of him whenever he would come over. Thank God he didn't visit too often. He later ended up in jail for child molestation and eventually hung himself. That was when I told my father who he was. My father was not the melodramatic type and just kind of sympathized with me and said, "I guess he had it coming to him."

Besides this contrary association with this child molester, my father was my rock and soul star of my life. I've seen so much of me in him. Unfortunately, he did not have a nurturing upbringing, as his mother gave him up for adoption and placed him in an orphanage. The story of his upbringing has remained a mystery. I did meet his sister in Thunder Bay, but she never did tell us her story.

After his passing in 2007, I came across his Holy Sacrament of Baptism and found that his father's name (my grandfather) was Adolph Love. I was so captivated by this that I decided to use his name as my alias for my writing and future stories. After all, it could have been my last name if my grandparents had married.

My dad didn't talk much about his upbringing, but I could sense it was disciplined and at the same time abusive. I can imagine growing up in a Roman Catholic orphanage was probably not all milk and honey. Yet he must have known love, as he came across as a very generous, loving, and sympathetic soul to all those who knew him.

In fact, I thought he was such a pushover at times when he could not say no to people, primarily my mother's siblings when they wanted his time. I vowed to never be like that, which is probably why I ended up with partners who were more on the assertive/aggressive side and emotionally unavailable.

My family had our own financial struggles. My father had various jobs as a truck driver and later worked for a car carrier and other major bus/train manufacturers as a welder's helper, until he had to retire due to emphysema, which later turned into COPD. Although he was more on the positive side of things, he also liked to complain about events and people in society, but he did it without prejudice.

When my dad was home and part of our family, it was so wonderful having him there. While he was a truck driver, he was home only periodically. Due to my insecurity and resentment of other people's demands on him, there were times when I felt neglected because he was always so busy doing stuff for others. But I knew in my heart that he loved me very much, and he was the only person that I could truly express my feelings to. He was just such a caring and generous soul who would do anything to help another.

When my mom and dad separated, I was around twelve years old. It was the saddest time of my life, and I didn't know how to cope with it. I hung around and acted out in not so constructive ways with people my age or older and just sort of drifted through life. He soon moved away to Thunder Bay, and I went to visit him as often as I could. It was a beautiful seven- or eight-hour drive to get there, and I loved every trip, especially the scenery. But still, he felt so distant from me, and I really did want to get to know him. We had some good times together and talked on the phone often.

When he became extremely sick from COPD and was in the hospital in TB, he asked me to come out there to be with him during his final days. I was overwhelmed, but my mother and I made the journey. After a few days of being by his side at the hospital, I had to leave, as I needed rest. My mom and I went back to the hotel room to sleep. I was called at around four in the morning and told that he had passed away. I was so guilt ridden for not being by his side when he passed. However, I now know from our spiritual connection and life after life that he is and forever will be with me.

My mother and I made the trip together in her van, and my partner had to stay with the girls and work. I did tell a few friends from our dance group where I was going. They were very empathetic, and I returned home to flowers and sympathy cards and their love. It was so nice to come back and know I had people who loved me.

CHAPTER 28

My Healing Journey&Life as a Victim and How I Became the Victor

"I have the Power to make Changes
– It is so comfortable to play victim, because it is
always someone else's fault. I have to stand on my
own two feet and take some responsibility"

Louise Hay – Affirmation Cards

As I've mentioned, I've always been a highly sensitive and intuitive person even though I was a shy, introverted person and found it difficult to be open and comfortable around people. I believed that I had an antisocial disorder and needed a crutch to give me courage to socialize. I later learned that this is part of being an empath and light worker. Most people don't realize that I had a reliance on drugs and alcohol, which I used in order to fit in. It gave me the courage I needed at certain times and later became my painkiller.

Besides all the shadows of dysfunction in my family of origin, the tendency toward addiction, jealousy, and vindictiveness were also character traits and probably caused the most pain in our lives. From what I can recall, these contributed, and still do to this day, to the blockage of our contentment and acceptance of one another.

Still, I like to believe that I overcame the horrible emotions of jealousy and resentment early on in life and realized that we are all made equal in the eyes of our creator. Through working on my insecurities, I've come to honor and respect those who have progressed themselves by advancing their education. I would have done the same back then if I had the financial means. In fact, I still consider myself a lifelong student of life and realize that experience is our best teacher.

As mentioned, life has not been a bed of roses for me and my family. Growing up in an addiction-filled, poverty-stricken, very dysfunctional family was disheartening. As a spiritual empath, I had to find ways to cope.

In my younger days, I hate to admit these ways were not very healthy or wholesome. I started smoking at age twelve and drinking alcohol and doing drugs at age thirteen. I became rebellious and lost, seeking love and acceptance in all the wrong places. Although I felt like I was in love with the people I dated, I learned that loving yourself first matters most. Quite frankly, I didn't know the difference between love and lust and only knew that I had a thirst for more love and acceptance and wanted connection with others.

Even my so-called friends would turn on me and were not very supportive. But I forgave them and will always love them. I even miss them and hope to someday have more time and energy to reconnect.

However, I have and can easily make new friends as I pursue my sacred path with my newfound passions and outlook on life.

Even though I participated in self-sabotage, I wanted so desperately to be healthy and whole. From the time I first became pregnant at sixteen, I strived to be healthy so that my children could have the best start in life. I immediately quit drinking and smoking. I exercised daily and read books on nutrition and how to live a positive life and be a better parent. I am so blessed to have three beautiful, healthy children, although they too had their bouts of mental dysfunction that required divine intervention and a lot of prayer, love, and patience.

In my prior ambitious life, I went into a health food business with my partner at the time, and we opened and operated a health food store in the eighties called Optimum Health. However, it was not an easy venture while working full-time. But it was another learning experience that I will treasure.

I read so many books and articles on vitamin and mineral supplements as well as herbs and essential oils that at times it became overwhelming. But I always believed that I was an expert and only wanted to share this knowledge with others.

Not only have I found that diet and exercise works well to keep us healthy, I also believe that taking supplements such as omega-3 and turmeric tremendously aide in reducing inflammation. Inflammation is the culprit that perpetuates the feelings of stiffness and exhaustion in fibromyalgia. A daily dose of rest and relaxation also does wonders for rejuvenating the muscles, joints, and tendons.

As mentioned throughout this memoir, I've read a lot of spiritual and self-help books. I once read—and it resonated with me so profoundly that it was a healing and ah-ha moment—that being able to forgive yourself and others and eliminating the guilt in your life will help you to heal and gain a greater understanding of where you came from and why you had to go through the lessons.

Over most of my life and especially the last few years, I felt something was missing. I needed to find a connection to my higher self. I am realizing and learning that love is the answer to our spiritual needs.

During the last ten years or so, I set out to find a spiritual life. I recently came across a metaphysical shop and decided to venture in. I was so in awe that they offered workshops on angel energy therapies, Reiki, crystal therapy, mediumship, and more. Over the last few years, I've attended these workshops as well as quantum touch and want so much to practice these. I've been told and believe that I am an energy healer and have the gift of divination. I plan to someday open my own practice and assist others on their healing journey with love and compassion.

I now have a life filled with hope, gratitude, compassion, and growth for a better future. I've been learning how to meditate and develop my intuitive abilities. I am ready for the wisdom and knowledge to come through my higher self. We are all connected to the divine power of our creator, source of all that is, God, and as energy, we are all connected.

I've purchased and read Louise Hay's *Wisdom Cards* that give me the wisdom and ability to "treat myself with unconditional love," and I "learned to forgive all my past experiences," even if they were unpleasant ones.

Another wonderful card deck is the *I Can Do It* cards; they have given me an enhanced sense of joy, power, and contentment.

My faith in healing my body really became solid when I watched the *You Can Heal Your Life* video.

I also purchased and read *The Universe Has Your Back* and really resonated with the affirmation "My Faith has the Power to turn trauma into Healing, Conflict into Growth and Fear into Love."

> If you can let anger subside, forgive yourself and others without guilt or shame and let fear be replaced with more hopefulness, you will easily tap into a momentum of Well-being. It will seem so easy; you will wonder why you didn't do it sooner and more often or had practiced it sooner.

As the old saying goes, if only I knew then what I know now, life could have been a lot smoother. But I know now that today is a gift and is the first day of the rest of my life.

As previously mentioned, I will continue to enjoy a dynamic lifestyle by including activities that bring me joy and calmness, such as yoga, meditation, dancing, golf that allows me to walk in nature, cleaning the house, and more. Some days I like to play a video with an exercise program, especially in our extreme cold, as I do live in Canada, the true north. I also enjoy traveling to warmer climates such as Mexico and Arizona.

I am looking forward to becoming a light worker to bring my light and love to others through this book and other avenues of energy-healing practices, including coaching through angel readings and writing with divine guidance.

While meditating on how to end this book, I came across a reading in *The Spiritual Journey—From Addiction to Recovery.* These were all short stories from recovering addicts. One of them included this message that resonated with me:

> While mediating you may find that small voice within you that will guide you to do something greater with your life. Listen to it and let it go, go with the flow, come out of your comfort zone. We have unlimited spiritual potential and we are being nudged to grow into it, to use it for the greater good. With this feeling we have become aware of a new level of receiving, of openness to the universe.

I would like to close with blessings from my *Blessing and Divination* cards:

> Just remember we are all blessed no matter what we achieve or don't achieve. Every experience enriches us and those around us in some way. All is a blessing in one form or another. Nothing is a mistake, for all serves a divine purpose. All is blessed.

Remember "The Blessing of Omnipresence" when doing meditation:

> Breathe in light and breathe out any unwanted thoughts. Dwelling on what has been, or might have been, serves no purpose. Feel the healing omnipresent light that surrounds and fills you. Focus on the present for it is blessed with infinite potential.

And to conclude, "The Blessing of Letting go: Namaste! Which means 'I honor the spirit in you which is also in me.'"

References and resources from my personal library:

- Dr. Wayne Dyer
  o *Being in Balance*
  o *The Shift*
  o *Secrets of Manifestation*
  o *Everyday Wisdom for Success*
  o *Excuses Begone*
- Louise Hay
- *You Can Heal Your Life*
- Doreen Virtue
  o *Don't Let Anyone Dull Your Sparkle*
  o *Assertive for Earth Angels*
  o *Angel Numbers*
  o *Angels of Abundance*
  o *Fairy* and various *Archangel* cards
- Dr. Judith Orloff, MD
  o *Guide to Intuitive Healing*
  o *Combatting Emotional Vampires* (online)
  o *The Power of Surrender* cards
- Lisa Rankin, MD
  o *Write Your Own Prescription*
- Esther and Jerry Hicks
  o *The Teachings of Abraham* (any)
- Christiane Northrup, MD
  o *The Wisdom of Menopause*
  o *Women's Bodies, Women's Wisdom*
- Rebecca Campbell
  o *Discover Your Cosmic Blueprint*
  o *Work Your Light Oracle* cards
- Jack Canfield and DD Watkins
  o *Living the Law of Attraction*
  o Gratitude Journal and Vision Board
- Rhonda Byrne
  o *The Secret, The Magic, Hero*

- Sylvia Brown (psychic medium)
  - o numerous books
- Ana Holub (from the *Daily OM*)
  - o *Heal Addictions with Forgiveness*
- Sara Wiseman (from the *Daily OM*)
  - o Release Yourself from Family Karma
  - o other short online courses
- Don Miguel Ruiz
  - o *The Voice of Knowledge*
  - o *The Four Agreements*
  - o *The Mastery of Love*
- Toni Carmine Salerno
  - o *Namaste—Blessing & Divination* cards
- Collette Baron-Reid
  - o *Remembering the Future*
  - o various card decks
- Radleigh Valentine
  - o *How to Be Your Own Genie*
  - o Certified Angel Card Reader (course)
  - o various card decks
- Winnipeg Regional Health Authority (WRHA)
  - o For definitions of Fibromyalgia

ACKNOWLEDGMENTS

Thank you to my childhood friends, Shelly, Julie and Norman, Michelle and Wayne, Kim and Greg; Donalda, Debbie and Rick; Karen and Lenard, who moved to BC; Alice and Don, Kim Lee, Colleen, Lisa, Frank, and all of the others in these families who've accepted me for who I am and given me courage to grow.

Thank you to my blood relatives and soul family—Aunt Flo and Auntie Marlene, my cousins Larry and Vern Morrissette and their families. My aunts and uncles, mom, my dad, and of course all my siblings who've shown me how to deal with my karma and life lessons. And of course, my mother, Rose, father, Vern, brothers, Barry, Vern, Andrew, and Greg, and my sister, Tammy. May you come to know your divine essence and may we all meet again on the other side.

Thank you to my former in-laws (now consider my outlaws, ha, ha, ha)—Betty, Rolly, Jill, Norman, Tod and Ed, Sheila, Barb and her family; my former mother-in-law Sandy (may she rest in peace), Georgie, Rod, Leanne, and their families. Thank you so much for your love and emotional support to me and my family.

Thank you to Joan, Laureen, and Brenda from my first real job and especially all the people I've worked with and who encourage me to succeed —Charles, Rod Sr., Rod Jr., Jamie, Diane, and Karen. Thank you for believing in my abilities and giving me opportunities to excel in them.

Thank you to the people from my work in the federal public sectors—Greg, Kathy, Don, Conchita, Sherry, and many others.

People from my provincial public sector jobs—Kitty, Brenda, Jack, Jeannette, Tony, Loren, Ken, Dan, Linda, Diane, Pat, Tracy, Donna, Estelle, Joe, and numerous others. And especially Linda, who is my encouragement.

Thank you to all the wonderful people at my last place of

employment at the Southern First Nations Network of Care, especially Ken, who has crossed my career path a few times, Trevor, Gladys, Karen, Sharon, Janine, and more.

Thank you so much for helping me succeed in my life and career.

And finally, thank you from the bottom of my heart to my new husband and soul mate, Henry, who is the most wonderful soul mate and friend one could ever ask for.

I would also like to thank Elma, who helped me immensely in editing this book and gave me the courage to pursue it. Thank you!

As taught by my mother when I was young and many spiritual advisors, we create our own reality. If I look back on my life, I can see that I was determined to make my life work and have what my heart desires. I recall writing resume after resume with cover letter and hoping to get that dream job, and although it seemed like hard work at the time, I ended up with a few wonderful opportunities. I recall dreaming about my soul mate, and I've had a few. You must remember that your desires may just be learning experiences to provide you lessons for your new desires and dreams to come.

Printed in the United States
By Bookmasters